TSI TEXAS SUCCESS INITIATIVE MATH PRACTICE TESTS

185 TSI Math Practice Problems and Solutions

TABLE OF CONTENTS

TEXAS SUCCESS INITIATIVE – MATH REVIEW:

TEXAS SUCCESS INITIATIVE – MATH PRACTICE TEST PROBLEMS:

TEXAS SUCCESS INITIATIVE – MATH REVIEW:

Coordinate geometry:

Midpoints:

For two points on a graph (x_1, y_1) and (x_2, y_2), the midpoint is: $(x_1 + x_2) \div 2$, $(y_1 + y_2) \div 2$

Slope:

In order to calculate the slope of a line, you need this formula: $y = mx + b$

m is the slope and b is the y intercept (the point at which the line crosses the y axis).

If two lines are perpendicular, the product of their slopes is equal to -1. If two lines are parallel, they will have the same slope.

Distance formula:

$$d = \sqrt{(x_2 - x_1)^2 + (y_2 - y_1)^2}$$

Exponent laws:

Same base numbers with different exponents:

If the base number is the same, and the problem asks you to multiply, you add the exponents. If the base number is the same, and the problem asks you to divide, you subtract the exponents.

Example: $4^2 \times 4^5 = 4^{(2 + 5)} = 4^7$

Different base numbers:

If the base numbers are different, you need to multiply the base numbers, but add the exponents.

Example: $(2x^3)(-4x^5) = -8x^8$

Fractions as exponents:

Place the base number inside the radical sign. The denominator of the exponent is the nth root of the radical, and the numerator is new exponent. Example: $x^{2/5} = (\sqrt[5]{x})^2$

Negative exponents:

Remove the negative sign on the exponent by expressing the number as a fraction, with 1 as the numerator. Example: $x^{-3} = \dfrac{1}{x^3}$

Fractions containing fractions:

Question: $\dfrac{x + \dfrac{1}{5}}{\dfrac{1}{x}} = ?$

Explanation: When you see fractions that have fractions within themselves, remember to treat the denominator as the division sign.

$$\dfrac{x + \dfrac{1}{5}}{\dfrac{1}{x}} = \left(x + \dfrac{1}{5} \right) \div \dfrac{1}{x}$$

Then invert and multiply the fractions as usual. In this case $\dfrac{1}{x}$ becomes $\dfrac{x}{1}$ when inverted, which is then simplified to x.

$$\left(x + \dfrac{1}{5} \right) \div \dfrac{1}{x} =$$

$$\left(x + \dfrac{1}{5} \right) \times x =$$

$$x^2 + \dfrac{x}{5}$$

Fractions containing radicals:

Tip: Eliminate the radical by squaring both sides of the equation.

Question: If $\dfrac{8}{\sqrt{x^2 - 12}} = 4$, then $x = ?$

<u>Explanation:</u> You may see fractions that contain radicals in the numerator or denominator. Eliminate the denominator of the fraction by multiplying both sides of the equation by the radical.

$$\frac{8}{\sqrt{x^2 - 12}} = 4$$

$$\frac{8}{\sqrt{x^2 - 12}} \times \sqrt{x^2 - 12} = 4 \times \sqrt{x^2 - 12}$$

$$8 = 4\sqrt{x^2 - 12}$$

Then eliminate the integer in front of the radical.

$$8 = 4\sqrt{x^2 - 12} =$$

$$8 \div 4 = (4\sqrt{x^2 - 12}) \div 4$$

$$2 = \sqrt{x^2 - 12}$$

Then eliminate the radical by squaring both sides of the equation, and solve for *x*.

$$2 = \sqrt{x^2 - 12} =$$

$$2^2 = (\sqrt{x^2 - 12})^2$$

$$4 = x^2 - 12$$

$$4 + 12 = x^2 - 12 + 12$$

$$16 = x^2$$

$$x = 4$$

Geometric reasoning:

Geometric reasoning questions cover the measurement of circles, triangles, cylinders, cones, or parallelograms.

<u>Area of circles:</u> $\pi \times r^2$ (radius squared)

Area of squares and rectangles: length × width

Area of triangles: (base × height) ÷ 2

Arcs: Arc length is the distance on the outside (or partial circumference) of a circle.

Chords: Chord length is always the straight line connecting the given points.

Circumference of a circle: π × diameter

diameter = radius × 2

Cone volume: (π × radius^2 × height) ÷ 3

Cylinder volume: $V = \pi r^2 h$

Explanation: To calculate the volume of a cylinder you take π times the radius squared times the height.

Hypotenuse length: hypotenuse length $C = \sqrt{A^2 + B^2}$

Explanation: The length of the hypotenuse is always the square root of the sum of the squares of the other two sides of the triangle.

Perimeter of squares and rectangles: (length × 2) + (width × 2)

Radians: $\theta = s \div r$

θ = the radians of the subtended angle
s = arc length
r = radius

$\pi \div 6$ × radians = 30°
$\pi \div 4$ × radians = 45°
$\pi \div 2$ × radians = 90°
π × radians = 180°
$\pi \times 2$ × radians = 360°

Inequalities:

Inequalities contain the less than or greater than signs.

Tip: In order to solve inequalities, deal with the whole numbers before dealing with the fractions.

Question:

$25 - \frac{2}{3}X > 21$, then $X < ?$

Explanation: Deal with the whole numbers on each side of the equation first.

$25 - {}^2/_3X > 21$

$(25 - 25) - {}^2/_3X > (21 - 25)$

$-{}^2/_3X > -4$

Then deal with the fraction.

$-{}^2/_3X > -4$

$3 \times -{}^2/_3X > -4 \times 3$

$-2X > -12$

Then deal with the remaining whole numbers.

$-2X > -12$

$-2X \div 2 > -12 \div 2$

$-X > -6$

Then deal with the negative number.

$-X > -6$

$-X + 6 > -6 + 6$

$-X + 6 > 0$

Finally, isolate the unknown variable as a positive number.

$-X + 6 > 0$

$-X + X + 6 > 0 + X$

$6 > X$

$X < 6$

Logarithmic functions:

Logarithmic functions are just another way of expressing exponents.

$x = \log_y Z$ is always the same as: $y^x = Z$

Polynomials – Solving for an unknown variable:

Polynomials are algebraic expressions that contain integers, variables, and variables which are raised to whole-number positive exponents.

Tip: You will certainly see problems involving polynomials on the exam. Be sure that you know these concepts well.

Question: If $3x - 2(x + 5) = -8$, then $x = $?

Explanation: To solve this type of problem, do multiplication of the items in parentheses first.

$3x - 2(x + 5) = -8$

$3x - 2x - 10 = -8$

Then deal with the integers by putting them on one side of the equation.

$3x - 2x - 10 + 10 = -8 + 10$

$3x - 2x = 2$

Then solve for x.

$3x - 2x = 2$

$1x = 2$

$x = 2$

Polynomials – "FOIL" Method:

Question: $(2x - 3y)^2 = $?

Explanation: When multiplying polynomials like this one, you should use the FOIL method.

This means that you multiply the terms two at a time from each of the two parts of the equation in the parentheses in this order:

First – Outside – Inside – Last

$(2x - 3y)^2 = (2x - 3y)(2x - 3y)$

So the first terms in each set of parentheses are $2x$ and $2x$

FIRST: $2x \times 2x = 4x^2$

The terms on the outside of each set of parentheses are $2x$ and $-3y$

OUTSIDE: $2x \times -3y = -6xy$

The terms on the inside of each set of parentheses are $-3y$ and $2x$

INSIDE: $-3y \times 2x = -6xy$

The last terms in each set of parentheses are $-3y$ and $-3y$

LAST: $-3y \times -3y = 9y^2$

Then we add all of the above parts together to get:

$4x^2 - 6xy - 6xy + 9y^2 =$

$4x^2 - 12xy + 9y^2$

Polynomials – Solving by division:

Question: $(x^2 - x - 6) \div (x - 3) = ?$

Explanation: In order to solve this type of problem, you must to long division of the polynomial.

$$
\begin{array}{r}
x + 2 \\
x - 3 \overline{)\, x^2 - x - 6 } \\
\underline{x^2 - 3x } \\
2x - 6 \\
\underline{2x - 6} \\
0
\end{array}
$$

Polynomial expressions that have more than two terms:

Question: Perform the operation: $(5ab - 6a)(3ab^3 - 4b^2 - 3a)$

Explanation: You might also see problems on the exam in which you have to carry out operations on polynomial expressions that have more than two terms.

Step 1 – Apply the distributive property of multiplication by multiplying the first term in the first set of parentheses by all of the items inside the second pair of parentheses. Then multiply the second term from the first set of parentheses by all of the items inside the second set of parentheses.

Step 2 – Add up the individual products in order to solve the problem.

$$(5ab - 6a)(3ab^3 - 4b^2 - 3a) =$$

$$(5ab \times 3ab^3) + (5ab \times -4b^2) + (5ab \times -3a) + (-6a \times 3ab^3) + (-6a \times -4b^2) + (-6a \times -3a) =$$

$$15a^2b^4 - 20ab^3 - 15a^2b - 18a^2b^3 + 24ab^2 + 18a^2$$

Probability:

For probability problems, your first step is to calculate how many items there are in total, before any are taken away.

Simply stated, probability can be expressed as a fraction, with the amount of chances as the numerator and the total items as the denominator. Probability can also be expressed as a percentage.

For more complex probability problems, you need two concepts: "sample space" and "event of interest."

S represents the sample space, and E represents the event of interest.

S is the amount of items in the total data set, and E is the possible number of outcomes.

For instance, what is the probability of drawing the ten of hearts from a pack of cards?

S is equal to 52 because there are 52 cards in a deck.

E is equal to 1 because there is only one ten of hearts.

The probability of event E is calculated by dividing the event into the sample space S: 1 / 52

Radicals (square roots):

You will see several problems involving radicals on the exam. Be sure that you know the following principles.

<u>Question 1 – Multiplication of radicals:</u>

$\sqrt{6} \times \sqrt{5} = ?$

<u>Explanation:</u> Multiply the numbers inside the square root signs first:

$6 \times 5 = 30$

Then put this result inside a square root symbol for your answer:

$\sqrt{30}$

Question 2 – Rationalizing radicals:

Express as a rational number: $\sqrt[3]{\dfrac{8}{27}}$

Explanation: You may see problems on the exam that ask you to rationalize a number or to express a radical number as a rational number. For these types of questions, you have to perform the necessary mathematical operations in order to remove the square root symbol. In the question above, you have to find the cube root of the numerator and denominator in order to eliminate the radical.

$$\sqrt[3]{\dfrac{8}{27}} = \sqrt[3]{\dfrac{2 \times 2 \times 2}{3 \times 3 \times 3}} = \dfrac{2}{3}$$

Question 3 – Factoring radicals:

$$\sqrt{32} + 2\sqrt{72} + 3\sqrt{18} = ?$$

Explanation: First you need to find the squared factors of the amounts inside the radical signs. Then simplify.

$$\sqrt{32} + 2\sqrt{72} + 3\sqrt{18} =$$

$$\sqrt{2 \times 16} + 2\sqrt{2 \times 36} + 3\sqrt{2 \times 9} =$$

$$4\sqrt{2} + (2 \times 6)\sqrt{2} + (3 \times 3)\sqrt{2} =$$

$$4\sqrt{2} + 12\sqrt{2} + 9\sqrt{2} = 25\sqrt{2}$$

Rational expressions:

On the algebra part of the exam, you may see fractions that contain rational expressions.

Remember that "rational expressions" means math problems that contain algebraic terms.

Question 1:

For some of these types of problems, you will have to add or subtract two fractions that contain rational expressions.

$$\dfrac{x^6}{x^2 - 4x} + \dfrac{4}{x} = ?$$

Explanation: To solve the problem, you need to find the lowest-common denominator, just like you would for any other type of problem involving the addition or subtraction of fractions.

$$\frac{x^6}{x^2 - 4x} + \frac{4}{x} =$$

$$\frac{x^6}{x^2 - 4x} + \left(\frac{4}{x} \times \frac{x - 4}{x - 4}\right) =$$

$$\frac{x^6}{x^2 - 4x} + \frac{4x - 16}{x^2 - 4x} =$$

$$\frac{x^6 + 4x - 16}{x^2 - 4x}$$

Question 2:

Here is another example of this type of problem, which asks you to multiply two fractions, both of which contain rational expressions.

$$\frac{4x^3}{3} \times \frac{3}{x^2} = ?$$

Explanation: To solve this problem, multiply the numerator of the first fraction by the numerator of the second fraction to calculate the numerator of the new fraction.

Then multiply the denominators in order to get the new denominator.

Finally, simplify as much as possible.

$$\frac{4x^3}{3} \times \frac{3}{x^2} = \frac{12x^3}{3x^2} = \frac{12x}{3} = 4x$$

Question 3:

You may also be asked to divide two fractions, both of which contain rational expressions.

$$\frac{5x + 5}{x^2} \div \frac{3x + 3}{x^3} = ?$$

Explanation: The first step in solving the problem is to invert and multiply by the second fraction.

Then cancel out the common factors in order to get your final result.

$$\frac{5x+5}{x^2} \div \frac{3x+3}{x^3} =$$

$$\frac{5x+5}{x^2} \times \frac{x^3}{3x+3} =$$

$$\frac{x^3(5x+5)}{x^2(3x+3)} =$$

$$\frac{5x^3(x+1)}{3x^2(x+1)} =$$

$$\frac{5x}{3}$$

Scientific notation:

Scientific notation means that you have to give the number as a multiple of 10^2, in other words, as a factor of 100.

So in scientific notation, the number 517 is: 5.17×10^2

Statistical analysis:

Mean:

The arithmetic mean is the average of a set of numbers. The mean is calculated by dividing the total of all of the numbers by the amount of items in the set.

Median:

The median is simply the middle value in the data set. Consider this data set: 12, 20, 3, 25, 30, 28, 18. First you have to put the numbers in the data set in the correct order from lowest to highest: 3, 12, 18, 20, 25, 28, 30. The median is the middle number in the set, which is 20 in this example.

Mode:

The mode is the number that appears the most often. For example, the number 5 appears four times in 1, 2, 5, 5, 5, 5, 8, 8, 9. Accordingly, 5 is the mode since it is the most frequent number in the data set.

If no number is duplicated, then we say that the data set has no mode.

Sometimes there are two figures that appear the same number of times. When this happens, we say that the data set is bimodal, and we assign two modes.

Range:

The range is calculated by subtracting the minimum value in the data set from the maximum value in the data set. In other words, the range tells you the spread of the data. For example, if the lowest number is a data set is 53 and the highest value is 84, the range is: $84 - 53 = 31$

Variance:

The variance measures the spread of the data around the arithmetic mean of the data set. The variance of a data set is calculated in four steps:

Step 1 – Calculate the arithmetic mean for the data set.

Step 2 – Find the "difference from the mean" for each item in the data set.

The "difference from the mean" is found by subtracting the mean from each value in the data set.

Step 3 – Square the "difference from the mean" for each item in the data set.

Step 4 – Calculate the mean of the squared figures derived from step 3 above to get the variance.

Standard deviation:

The standard deviation is calculated by taking the square root of the variance.

Percentile:

The percentile for an observation x is found by dividing the number of observations less than x by the total number of observations and then multiplying this quantity by 100.

TEXAS SUCCESS INITIATIVE – MATH PRACTICE

Practice Problems - Elementary Algebra, Inequalities, and Word Problems:

1) $(5x + 7y) + (3x - 9y) = ?$

2) Simplify the following: $(5x^2 + 3x - 4) - (6x^2 - 5x + 8)$

3) Factor the following: $x^2 + x - 20$

4) $(x - 4y)^2 = ?$

5) If $4x - 3(x + 2) = -3$, then $x = ?$

6) $(x^2 - x - 12) \div (x - 4) = ?$

7) What is the value of the expression $2x^2 + 3xy - y^2$ when $x = 3$ and $y = -3$?

8) $(x - y)(3x + y) = ?$

9) $(x^2 - 4) \div (x + 2) = ?$

10) If $5x - 2(x + 3) = 0$, then $x = ?$

11) Simplify the following equation: $(x + 3y)^2$

12) $(x + 3y)(x - y) = ?$

13) What is the value of the expression $6x^2 - xy + y^2$ when $x = 5$ and $y = -1$?

14) $20 - \frac{3}{4}X > 17$, then $X < ?$

15) $(x - 4)(3x + 2) = ?$

16) $100 - \frac{4}{5}X > 16$, then $X < ?$

17) If $7x - 5(x + 1) = -3$, then $x = ?$

18) Simplify: $(x - 2y)(2x - y)$

19) $(2x - y)(x - 3y) = ?$

20) What is the value of the expression $3x^2 - xy + y^2$ when $x = 2$ and $y = -2$?

21) $32 - \frac{1}{4}X > 8$, then $X < ?$

22) $(2x + 5y)^2 = ?$

23) If $5x - 4(x + 2) = -2$, then $x = ?$

24) What is the value of the expression $x^2 - xy + y^2$ when $x = 4$ and $y = -3$?

25) Simplify: $(x - y)(x + y)$

26) Factor the following: $2xy - 8x^2y + 6y^2x^2$

27) $(x + 3) - (4 - x) = ?$

28) Simplify the following: $(4x^2 - 5x - 3) - (x^2 + 10x)$

29) If $x - 1 > 0$ and $y = x - 1$, then $y > ?$

30) If $x - 5 < 0$ and $y < x + 10$, then $y < ?$

31) What are the values of x and y where $x| y - 1 | < 0$?
A. $x < 1$ and $y \neq 0$
B. $x < 0$ and $y \neq 1$
C. $x \neq 0$ and $y < 0$
D. $x \neq 1$ and $y < 0$

32) A class contains 20 students. On Tuesday 5% of the students were absent. On Wednesday 20% of the students were absent. How many more students were absent on Wednesday than on Tuesday?

33) Farmer Brown owns a herd of cattle. This year, his herd consisted of 250 cows. Then he sold 60% of his herd. How many cows does he have left?

34) Three people are going to contribute money to a charity. Person A will provide one-third of the money. Person B will contribute one-half of the money. What fraction represents Person C's contribution of money for the project?

35) The snowfall for November was 5 inches more than for December. If the total snowfall for November and December was 35 inches for the two months, what was the snowfall for November?

36) A museum counts its visitors each day and rounds each daily figure up or down to the nearest 10 people. 104 people visit the museum on Monday, 86 people visit the museum on Tuesday, and 81 people visit the museum on Wednesday. What amount represents the number of visitors to the museum for the three days, after rounding?

37) Mount Pleasant is 15,138 feet high. Mount Glacier is 9,927 feet high. What is the best estimate of the difference between the altitudes of the two mountains to the nearest thousand?

38) John is measuring plant growth as part of a botany experiment. Last week, his plant grew 7¾ inches, but this week his plant grew 10½ inches. By how much did this week's growth surpass last week's?

39) At the beginning of a class, one-fourth of the students leave to attend band practice. Later, one half of the remaining students leave to go to PE. If there were 15 students remaining in the class at the end, how many students were in the class at the beginning?

40) Tom bought a shirt on sale for $12. The original price of the shirt was $15. What was the percentage of the discount on the sale?

41) Shania is entering a talent competition which has three events. The third event (C) counts three times as much as the second event (B), and the second event counts twice as much as the first event (A). What equation, expressed only in terms of variable A, can be used to calculate Shania's final score for the competition?

42) Mark's final grade for a course is based on the grades from two tests, A and B. Test A counts toward 35% of his final grade. Test B counts toward 65% of his final grade. What equation is used to calculate Mark's final grade for this course?

43) If A represents the number of apples purchased at 20 cents each and B represents the number of bananas purchased at 25 cents each, what equation represents the total value of the purchase?

44) Two people are going to work on a job. The first person will be paid $7.25 per hour. The second person will be paid $10.50 per hour. If A represents the number of hours the first person will work, and B represents the number of hours the second person will work, what equation represents the total cost of the wages for this job?

45) The price of socks is $2 per pair and the price of shoes is $25 per pair. Anna went shopping for socks and shoes, and she paid $85 in total. In this purchase, she bought 3 pairs of shoes. How many pairs of socks did she buy?

46) A car travels at 60 miles per hour. The car is currently 240 miles from Denver. How long will it take for the car to get to Denver?

47) The Smith family is having lunch in a diner. They buy hot dogs and hamburgers to eat. The hot dogs cost $2.50 each, and the hamburgers cost $4 each. They buy 3 hamburgers. They also buy hot dogs. The total value of their purchase is $22. How many hot dogs did they buy?

48) A hockey team had 50 games this season and lost 20 percent of them. How many games did the team win?

49) In a batch of 4000 computer chips, $^1/_{80}$ was defective. What is the ratio of defective chips to non–defective chips?

50) The university bookstore is having a sale. Course books can be purchased for $40 each, or 5 books can be purchased for a total of $150. How much would a student save on each book if he or she purchases 5 books?

Solutions - Elementary Algebra, Inequalities, and Word Problems:

1) The correct answer is: $8x - 2y$

First perform the operations on the parentheses.

$(5x + 7y) + (3x - 9y) =$
$5x + 7y + 3x - 9y$

Then place the x and y terms together.

$5x + 3x + 7y - 9y$

Finally, add or subtract the x and y terms.

$5x + 3x + 7y - 9y =$
$8x - 2y$

2) The correct answer is: $-x^2 + 8x - 12$

Remember to perform the operations on the parentheses first and to be careful with the negatives.

$(5x^2 + 3x - 4) - (6x^2 - 5x + 8) = 5x^2 + 3x - 4 - 6x^2 + 5x - 8$

Then place the x and y terms together.

$5x^2 - 6x^2 + 3x + 5x - 4 - 8$

Finally, add or subtract the like terms.

$5x^2 - 6x^2 + 3x + 5x - 4 - 8 = -x^2 + 8x - 12$

3) The correct answer is: $(x + 5)(x - 4)$

We know that for any problem like this, the answer will be in the format: $(x + ?)(x - ?)$

We need to have a plus sign in one set of parentheses and a minus sign in the other set of parentheses because 20 is negative, and we can get a negative number in problems like this only if we multiply a negative and a positive.

We also know that the factors of 20 need to be one number different than each other because the middle term is x, in other words $1x$. The only factors of twenty that meet this criterion are 4 and 5.

Therefore the answer is $(x + 5)(x - 4)$

4) The correct answer is: $x^2 - 8xy + 16y^2$

$(x - 4y)^2 = (x - 4y)(x - 4y)$

For problems like this one, you need to use the FOIL method.

"FOIL" meals that you multiply the terms in this order: First – Outside – Inside – Last

FIRST: Multiply the first term from the first set of parentheses with the first term from the second set of parentheses.

$x \times x = x^2$

OUTSIDE: Multiply the first term from the first set of parentheses with the second term from the second set of parentheses.

$x \times -4y = -4xy$

INSIDE: Multiply the second term from the first set of parentheses with the first term from the second set of parentheses.

$-4y \times x = -4xy$

LAST: Multiply the second term from the first set of parentheses with the second term from the second set of parentheses.

$-4y \times -4y = 16y^2$

Then we add all of the above parts together to get: $x^2 - 8xy + 16y^2$

5) The correct answer is: 3

To solve this type of problem, do multiplication of the items in parentheses first.

$4x - 3(x + 2) = -3$
$4x - 3x - 6 = -3$

Then deal with the integers by putting them on one side of the equation.

$4x - 3x - 6 + 6 = -3 + 6$
$4x - 3x = 3$

Then solve for x.

$4x - 3x = 3$
$x = 3$

6) The correct answer is: $(x + 3)$

In order to solve this type of problem, you must do long division of the polynomial.

$$\begin{array}{r}
x + 3 \\
x - 4 \overline{)\, x^2 - x - 12\,} \\
\underline{x^2 - 4x} \\
3x - 12 \\
\underline{3x - 12} \\
0
\end{array}$$

7) The correct answer is: −18

To solve this problem, put in the values for x and y and multiply.

Remember to be careful when multiplying negative numbers.

$2x^2 + 3xy - y^2 =$
$(2 \times 3^2) + (3 \times 3 \times -3) - (-3^2) =$
$(2 \times 3 \times 3) + (3 \times 3 \times -3) - (-3 \times -3) =$
$(2 \times 9) + (3 \times -9) - (9) =$
$18 + (-27) - 9 =$
$18 - 27 - 9 =$
-18

8) The correct answer is: $3x^2 - 2xy - y^2$

Use the FOIL method: $(x - y)(3x + y) = ?$

FIRST: $x \times 3x = 3x^2$
OUTSIDE: $x \times y = xy$
INSIDE: $-y \times 3x = -3xy$
LAST: $-y \times y = -y^2$

Then add all of the above once you have completed FOIL.

$3x^2 + xy + -3xy + -y^2 =$
$3x^2 + xy - 3xy - y^2 =$
$3x^2 - 2xy - y^2$

9) The correct answer is: $x - 2$

For problems like this, look at the integers in the equation: $(x^2 - 4) \div (x + 2) = ?$

In this problem the integers are −4 and 2. We know that we have to divide −4 by 2 because the dividend is $(x + 2)$.

$-4 \div 2 = -2$

We also know that we have to divide x^2 by x, because these are the first terms in each set of parentheses: $x^2 \div x = x$

Now combine the two parts: $-2 + x = x - 2$

You can check your result as follows: $(x + 2)(x - 2) = x^2 - 2x + 2x - 4 = x^2 - 4$

10) The correct answer is: 2

Do the multiplication of the items in parentheses first.

$5x - 2(x + 3) = 0$
$5x - 2x - 6 = 0$

Put the integers to one side of the equation.

$5x - 2x - 6 + 6 = 0 + 6$
$3x = 6$

Then solve for x.

$3x = 6$
$x = 6 \div 3$
$x = 2$

11) The correct answer is: $x^2 + 6xy + 9y^2$

"Simplify" means that you have to state the equation in the fewest possible terms.

You simply $(x + 3y)^2$ by using the FOIL method.

$(x + 3y)(x + 3y)$

FIRST: $x \times x = x^2$

OUTSIDE: $x \times 3y = 3xy$

INSIDE: $3y \times x = 3xy$

LAST: $3y \times 3y = 9y^2$

Then we add all of the above parts together to get:

$x^2 + 3xy + 3xy + 9y^2 =$

$x^2 + 6xy + 9y^2$

12) The correct answer is: $x^2 + 2xy - 3y^2$

$(x + 3y)(x - y) = ?$

FIRST: $x \times x = x^2$

OUTSIDE: $x \times -y = -xy$

INSIDE: $3y \times x = 3xy$

LAST: $3y \times -y = -3y^2$

Then add all of the above together.

$x^2 - xy + 3xy - 3y^2 = x^2 + 2xy - 3y^2$

13) The correct answer is: 156

Substitute the values for x and y and multiply. Remember to be careful when multiplying negative numbers.

$6x^2 - xy + y^2 =$
$(6 \times 5^2) - (5 \times -1) + (-1^2) =$
$(6 \times 5 \times 5) - (-5) + 1 =$
$(6 \times 25) + 5 + 1 =$
$150 + 5 + 1 =$
156

14) The correct answer is: 4

In order to solve inequalities, deal with the whole numbers on each side of the equation first.

$20 - \frac{3}{4}X > 17$
$(20 - 20) - \frac{3}{4}X > (17 - 20)$
$-\frac{3}{4}X > -3$

Then deal with the fraction.

$-\frac{3}{4}X > -3$
$4 \times -\frac{3}{4}X > -3 \times 4$
$-3X > -12$

Then deal with the remaining whole numbers.

$-3X > -12$
$-3X \div 3 > -12 \div 3$
$-X > -4$

Then deal with the negative number.

$-X > -4$
$-X + 4 > -4 + 4$
$-X + 4 > 0$

Finally, isolate the unknown variable as a positive number.

$-X + 4 > 0$
$-X + X + 4 > 0 + X$
$4 > X$
$X < 4$

15) The correct answer is: $3x^2 - 10x - 8$

Here is another problem to help you practice the FOIL method: $(x - 4)(3x + 2) = ?$

FIRST: $x \times 3x = 3x^2$
OUTSIDE: $x \times 2 = 2x$
INSIDE: $-4 \times 3x = -12x$
LAST: $-4 \times 2 = -8$

Then add all of the above together.

$3x^2 + 2x + -12x + -8 =$
$3x^2 + 2x - 12x - 8 =$
$3x^2 - 10x - 8$

16) The correct answer is: $X < 105$

First get the whole numbers onto one side of the equation.

$100 - \,^4/_5X > 16$
$100 - 100 - \,^4/_5X > 16 - 100$
$-\,^4/_5X > -84$

Then eliminate the fraction.

$-\,^4/_5X > -84$
$5 \times -\,^4/_5X > -84 \times 5$
$-4X > -420$

Then deal with the remaining whole numbers.

Tip: Remember that if you are multiplying or dividing by a negative number in any inequality problem, you have to reverse the direction of the inequality symbol.

$-4X > -420$
$-4X \div -4 > -420 \div -4$
$X < 105$

17) The correct answer is: 1

Do multiplication of the items in parentheses first.

$7x - 5(x + 1) = -3$
$7x - 5x - 5 = -3$

Then get the integers to one side of the equation.

$7x - 5x - 5 + 5 = -3 + 5$
$7x - 5x = 2$

Then solve for x.

$2x = 2$
$x = 1$

18) The correct answer is: $2x^2 - 5xy + 2y^2$

Simplify: $(x - 2y)(2x - y)$

FIRST: $x \times 2x = 2x^2$
OUTSIDE: $x \times -y = -xy$
INSIDE: $-2y \times 2x = -4xy$
LAST: $-2y \times -y = 2y^2$

Then add all of the above once you have completed FOIL.

$2x^2 + -xy + -4xy + 2y^2 =$
$2x^2 - xy - 4xy + 2y^2 =$
$2x^2 - 5xy + 2y^2$

19) The correct answer is: $2x^2 - 7xy + 3y^2$

$(2x - y)(x - 3y) = ?$

FIRST: $2x \times x = 2x^2$
OUTSIDE: $2x \times -3y = -6xy$
INSIDE: $-y \times x = -xy$
LAST: $-y \times -3y = 3y^2$

You will know by now that the last step is to add the terms together.

$2x^2 + -6xy + -xy + 3y^2 =$
$2x^2 - 7xy + 3y^2$

20) The correct answer is: 20

Put in the values for x and y and multiply.

$3x^2 - xy + y^2 =$
$(3 \times 2^2) - (2 \times -2) + (-2^2) =$
$(3 \times 2 \times 2) - (2 \times -2) + (-2 \times -2) =$
$(3 \times 4) - (2 \times -2) + (4) =$
$12 - (-4) + 4 =$
$12 + 4 + 4 =$
20

21) The correct answer is: 96

Remember to deal with the whole numbers on each side of the equation first.

$32 - {}^1/_4X > 8$
$(32 - 32) - {}^1/_4X > (8 - 32)$
$-{}^1/_4X > -24$

Then deal with the fraction.

$-{}^1/_4X > -24$
$4 \times -{}^1/_4X > -24 \times 4$
$-X > -96$

Then deal with the negative number.

$-X > -96$
$-X + 96 > -96 + 96$
$-X + 96 > 0$

Finally, isolate the unknown variable as a positive number.

$-X + 96 > 0$
$-X + X + 96 > 0 + X$
$96 > X$
$X < 96$

22) The correct answer is: $4x^2 + 20xy + 25y^2$

$(2x + 5y)^2 = (2x + 5y)(2x + 5y)$

FIRST: $2x \times 2x = 4x^2$
OUTSIDE: $2x \times 5y = 10xy$
INSIDE: $5y \times 2x = 10xy$
LAST: $5y \times 5y = 25y^2$

Then we add all of the above terms together to get: $4x^2 + 20xy + 25y^2$

23) The correct answer is: 6

$5x - 4(x + 2) = -2$

$5x - 4x - 8 = -2$

$x - 8 = -2$

$x - 8 + 8 = -2 + 8$

$x = 6$

24) The correct answer is: 37

Substitute the values for x and y and multiply.

$x^2 - xy + y^2 =$
$(4^2) - (4 \times -3) + (-3^2) =$
$(4 \times 4) - (4 \times -3) + (-3 \times -3) =$
$16 - (-12) + (9) =$
$16 + 12 + 9 = 37$

25) The correct answer is: $x^2 - y^2$

Simplify: $(x - y)(x + y)$

FIRST: $x \times x = x^2$
OUTSIDE: $x \times y = xy$
INSIDE: $-y \times x = -xy$
LAST: $-y \times y = -y^2$

Then add all of the above terms.

$x^2 + xy + -xy - y^2 = x^2 - y^2$

26) The correct answer is: $2xy(1 - 4x + 3xy)$

In order to factor an equation, you must figure out what variables are common to each term of the equation. Let's look at this equation:

$2xy - 8x^2y + 6y^2x^2$

We can see that each term contains x. We can also see that each term contains y. So now let's factor out xy.

$2xy - 8x^2y + 6y^2x^2 =$
$xy(2 - 8x + 6xy)$

Then think about integers. We can see that all of the terms inside the parentheses are divisible by 2. Now let's factor out the 2. In order to do this, we divide each term inside the parentheses by 2.

$xy(2 - 8x + 6xy) =$
$2xy(1 - 4x + 3xy)$

27) The correct answer is: $2x - 1$

This question is asking you to simplify the terms in the parentheses. First you should look to see if there is any subtraction or if any of the numbers are negative. In this problem, the second part of the equation is subtracted. So we need to do the operation on the second set of parentheses first.

$(x + 3) - (4 - x) =$
$x + 3 - 4 + x$

Now simplify for the integers and common variable.

$x + 3 - 4 + x =$
$x + x + 3 - 4 =$
$2x - 1$

28) The correct answer is: $3x^2 - 15x - 3$

Follow the same steps as in the previous problem, performing the operation on the second set of parentheses as your first step

$(4x^2 - 5x - 3) - (x^2 + 10x) =$
$(4x^2 - 5x - 3) - x^2 - 10x$

Then we can remove the remaining parentheses.

$(4x^2 - 5x - 3) - x^2 - 10x =$
$4x^2 - 5x - 3 - x^2 - 10x$

Now simplify.

$4x^2 - 5x - 3 - x^2 - 10x =$
$4x^2 - x^2 - 5x - 10x - 3 =$
$3x^2 - 15x - 3$

29) The correct answer is: $y > 0$

Notice that both equations contain $x - 1$ in this inequality problem

Therefore, we can substitute y for $x - 1$ in the first equation:

$x - 1 > 0$
$x - 1 = y$
$y > 0$

30) The correct answer is: 15

You should first solve the equation for *x*.

$x - 5 < 0$
$x - 5 + 5 < 0 + 5$
$x < 5$

Now solve for *y* by replacing *x* with its value.

$y < x + 10$
$y < 5 + 10$
$y < 15$

31) The correct answer is: B

When you see numbers between lines like this $| y - 1 |$, you are being asked the absolute value. Absolute value is always zero or a positive number. So for this question:

$| y - 1 |$ will be a positive number, unless $y = 1$

In other words, if $y = 1$, then $| y - 1 | = | 1 - 1 | = 0$

So if *y* is 1, this would result in a final product of zero, because any number that is multiplied by zero is always equal to zero.

Accordingly, we know that *y* must not be equal to 1.

Therefore, in order for the final product to be less than zero, *x* must also be a negative number. So $x < 0$

32) The correct answer is: 3 students

Figure out the amount of absences for the two days and then subtract.

Tuesday's absences: $20 × 5\% = 1$

Wednesday's absences: $20 × 20\% = 4$

$4 - 1 = 3$

33) The correct answer is: 100

$250 × .60 = 150$ cows sold

$250 - 150 = 100$ cows left

34) The correct answer is: 1/6

The three people make up the whole contribution by paying in together, so the sum of contributions from all three people must be equal to 100%, simplified to 1.

A + B + C = 1

1/3 + 1/2 + C = 1

Now find the lowest common denominator of the fractions.

2/6 + 3/6 + C = 1

Therefore, C = 1/6

35) The correct answer is: 20 inches

Subtract the difference in snowfall between the two months from the total snowfall for the two months, and then divide by 2 in order to get the December snowfall.

35 – 5 = 30

30 ÷ 2 = 15

Now add back the excess for November to get the total for November.

15 + 5 = 20

36) The correct answer is: 270

A basic guideline for rounding is that 5 or more is rounded up, while 4 or less is rounded down.

Do the rounding for each day separately (before doing the addition) because this is stipulated in the problem. Then add together to solve the problem.

104 Rounded to 100

86 Rounded to 90

81 Rounded to 80

100 + 90 + 80 = 270

37) The correct answer is: 5,000 feet

Subtract the two amounts and then do the rounding. 15,138 – 9,927 = 5,211 (Rounded to 5,000)

Check by rounding the individual amounts as follows: 15,000 – 10,000 = 5,000

38) The correct answer is: 2¾ inches

This is essentially a mixed number problem. Here you can covert the fraction to decimals to make the subtraction easier.

$10\frac{1}{2} - 7\frac{3}{4} = 10.5 - 7.75 = 2.75 = 2\frac{3}{4}$

39) The correct answer is: 40 students

You need to create an equation to set out the facts of this problem. We will say that the total number of students is variable S.

$15 = (S - \frac{1}{4}S) \times \frac{1}{2}$

$15 = \frac{3}{4}S \times \frac{1}{2}$

$15 = \frac{3}{8}S$

$15 \times 8 = \frac{3}{8}S \times 8$

$120 = 3S$

$S = 40$

40) The correct answer is: 20%

In order to calculate a discount, you must first determine how much the item was marked down.

$15 - 12 = 3$

Then divide the mark down by the original price.

$3 \div 15 = 0.20$

Finally, convert the decimal to a percentage.

$0.20 = 20\%$

41) The correct answer is: 9A

Final Score = A + B + C

B = 2A

C = 3B = 3 × 2A = 6A

Now express the original equation in terms of A:

A + B + C = A + 2A + 6A = 9A

42) The correct answer is: .35A + .65B

The two tests are being given different percentages, so each assignment needs to have its own variable.

A for test A
B for test B

So the value of test A is .35A
The value of test B is .65B

The final grade is the sum of the values of these two variables: .35A + .65B

43) The correct answer is: .20A + .25B

Remember that each item needs to have its own variable. A is for apples and B for bananas. So the total value of the apples is .20A and the total value of the bananas is .25B

The total value of the purchase is the sum of the values of these two variables.

.20A + .25B

44) The correct answer is: (7.25A + 10.50B)

The two people are working at different per hour costs, so each person needs to have an individual variable.

A for the number of hours for the first person
B for the number of hours for the second person

So the equation for wages for the first person is: $(7.25 \times A)$
The equation for the wages for the second person is: $(10.50 \times B)$

The total cost of the wages for this job is the sum of the wages of these two people.

$(7.25 \times A) + (10.50 \times B) = (7.25A + 10.50B)$

45) The correct answer is: 5 pairs

Let's say that the number of pairs of socks is S and the number of pairs of shoes is H.

Now let's make an equation to express the above problem.

$(S \times \$2) + (H \times \$25) = \$85$

We know that the number of pairs of shoes is 3, so let's put that in the equation and solve it.

$(S \times \$2) + (H \times \$25) = \$85$
$(S \times \$2) + (3 \times \$25) = \$85$

$(S × \$2) + \$75 = \$85$
$(S × \$2) + 75 − 75 = \$85 − \$75$
$(S × \$2) = \$10$
$\$2S = \$10$
$\$2S ÷ 2 = \$10 ÷ 2$
$S = 5$

46) The correct answer is: 4 hours

Remember to read questions like this one very carefully. If the car travels at 60 miles an hour and needs to go 240 more miles, we need to divide the miles to travel by the miles per hour.

miles to travel ÷ miles per hour = time remaining

So if we substitute the values from the question, we get:

$240 ÷ 60 = 4$

In other words, the total time is 4 hours.

47) The correct answer: 4 hot dogs

The number of hot dogs is D and the number of hamburgers is H.

Here is the equation to express the problem: $(D × \$2.50) + (H × \$4) = \$22$

We know that the number of hamburgers is 3, so put that in the equation and solve it.

$(D × \$2.50) + (H × \$4) = \$22$
$(D × \$2.50) + (3 × \$4) = \$22$
$(D × \$2.50) + 12 = \$22$
$(D × \$2.50) + 12 − 12 = \$22 − 12$
$(D × \$2.50) = \$10$
$\$2.50D = \$10$
$\$2.50D ÷ \$2.50 = \$10 ÷ \$2.50$
$D = 4$

48) The correct answer is: 40

First of all, we have to calculate the percentage of games won. If the team lost 20 percent of the games, we know that the team won the remaining 80 percent.

Now do the long multiplication:

```
    50
×  .80
 ─────
  40.0
```

49) The correct answer is: $^{50}/_{3950}$

Take the total number of chips times the fraction of defective chips in order to calculate the amount of defective chips:

$4000 \times {}^{1}/_{80} =$
$4000 \div 80 =$
50 (This number becomes the numerator of the ratio.)

In order to determine the amount of non–defective chips for the denominator of the ratio, deduct the amount of defective chips from the total number of chips:

$4000 - 50 = 3950$

So the answer is $^{50}/_{3950}$

50) The correct answer is: $10

First divide the total price for the multi–purchase by the number of items. In this case: $150 \div 5 = $30 for each of the five books.

Then subtract this amount from the original price to get your answer:

$40 - $30 = $10

Practice Problems for Intermediate Algebra

Polynomials, Exponents, Roots, Radicals, Rational Expressions, and Functions:

1) Express the following number in scientific notation: 625

2) $8^7 \times 8^3 = ?$

3) $5^8 \div 5^2 = ?$

4) $\sqrt{5}$ is equivalent to what number in exponential notation?

5) Simplify: $\sqrt{7} + 2\sqrt{7}$

6) $\sqrt{2} \times \sqrt{3} = ?$

7) $\sqrt{8} \times \sqrt{2} = ?$

8) If $5 + 5(3\sqrt{x} + 4) = 55$, then $\sqrt{x} = ?$

9) Express the equation $2^5 = 32$ as a logarithmic function.

10) $x^{-7} = ?$

11) $\dfrac{5x^3}{4} \times \dfrac{7}{x^2} = ?$

12) $(-3x)(-6x^4) = ?$

13) $\dfrac{x^2 + 8x + 12}{x^2 + 8x + 16} \times \dfrac{x^2 + 4x}{x^2 + 11x + 30} = ?$

14) $\dfrac{3}{x^2 + 2x + 1} + \dfrac{5}{x^2 + x} = ?$

15) $3 = -\dfrac{1}{8}x$, then $x = ?$

16) $\sqrt{4x - 4} = 6$, then $x = ?$

17) $\dfrac{7x+7}{x} \div \dfrac{4x+4}{x^2} = ?$

18) What figure should be placed inside the parentheses? $49x^8 = 7x(\ \ )$

19) $(4x^8 + 5x^5 - 7) - (-6x^5 + 5x^8 - 7) = ?$

20) $\dfrac{2}{3x} = \dfrac{?}{9x^2}$

21) Find the lowest common denominator and express as one fraction: $\dfrac{8}{x} + \dfrac{3}{x+2}$

22) $B = \dfrac{1}{3}CD$ Express in the following form: $D =$

23) What are two possible values of x for the following equation? $6x^2 + 16x + 8 = 0$

24) Simplify: $\dfrac{x^2}{x^{-8}}$

25) If $W = \dfrac{XY}{Z}$, then $Z = ?$

26) $\dfrac{2}{15x} - \dfrac{4}{21x^2} = ?$

27) $A = \dfrac{1}{2}(B+C)d$, if $A = 120$, $B = 13$, $d = 8$, then $C = ?$

28) Perform the operation: $10ab^5(5ab^7 - 4b^3 - 10a)$

29) The sum of twice a number and 8 less than the number is the same as the difference between –28 and the number. What is the number?

30) Perform the operation. Then simplify: $\dfrac{z^2 + 7z + 10}{z^2 + 13z + 40} \div \dfrac{z+8}{z^2 + 16z + 64}$

31) Simplify: $\dfrac{x+\dfrac{1}{x}}{\dfrac{1}{x}}$

32) If $\dfrac{3a}{10}+9=12, a=?$

33) If $\dfrac{18}{\sqrt{x^2+4}}=6$, then $x=?$

34) Express as a rational number: $\sqrt[3]{\dfrac{64}{125}}$

35) What is the value of a when $\dfrac{b^2-ab+24}{b-12}=b-2?$

36) $125^{-\frac{2}{3}}=?$

37) If $\dfrac{20}{\sqrt{x^2+7}}=5$, then $x^2=?$

38) Rationalize the denominator: $\sqrt{\dfrac{16}{3}}$

39) What is the product of $(\sqrt{2}-5\sqrt{5})$ and $(3\sqrt{2}-4\sqrt{5})?$

40) For all $x\neq0$ and $y\neq0$, $\dfrac{4x}{\frac{1}{xy}}=?$

41) $64^{\frac{3}{2}}=?$

42) Simplify: $\dfrac{\sqrt{75}}{3}+\dfrac{5\sqrt{5}}{6}$

43) $\dfrac{\sqrt{36}}{3} + 5\dfrac{\sqrt{5}}{9} = ?$

44) $\sqrt{18} + 4\sqrt{75} + 5\sqrt{27} = ?$

45) $(4x^2 + 3x + 5)(6x^2 - 8) = ?$

46) Factor the following equation: $6xy - 12x^2y - 24y^2x^2$

47) $\sqrt{4x^8}\,\sqrt{6x^4} = ?$

48) $\sqrt{-9} = ?$

49) Convert $3^5 = 243$ to the equivalent logarithmic expression.

50) Which one of the following is a solution to the following ordered pairs of equations:
$y = -2x - 1$
$y = x - 4$

A) (0, 1)
B) (1, 3)
C) (4, 0)
D) (1, -3)

51) Find the value of the following:

$$\sum_{x=2}^{4} x + 1$$

52) $\dfrac{a^3/ab}{b/5b^2} = ?$

53) What is the value of Y that is missing from the chart?

X	Y
2	4
4	16
6	
8	64
10	100

54) $(x^2 \div y^3)^3 = ?$

55) $2^4 \times 2^2 = ?$

56) $(-3x^2 + 7x + 2)(x^2 - 5) = ?$

57) $(A^5 \div A^2)^4 = ?$

58) If Д is a special operation defined by $(x \text{ Д } y) = (2x \div 4y)$ and $(8 \text{ Д } y) = 16$, then $y = ?$

59) For the two functions $f_1(x)$ and $f_2(x)$, tables of values are given below. What is the value of $f_2(f_1(2))$?

x	$f_1(x)$	x	$f_2(x)$
1	3	2	4
2	5	3	9
3	7	4	16
4	9	5	25
5	11	6	36

60) For the functions $f_2(x)$ listed below, x and y are integers greater than 1. If $f_1(x) = x^2$, which of the functions has the greatest value for $f_1(f_2(x))$?
A. $f_2(x) = x/y$
B. $f_2(x) = y/x$
C. $f_2(x) = xy$
D. $f_2(x) = x - y$

Solutions – Intermediate Algebra Problems:

1) The correct answer is: 6.25×10^2

Scientific notation means that you have to give the number as a multiple of 10^2, in other words, as a factor of 100.

We know that 625 divided by 100 is 6.25.

So the answer is 6.25×10^2.

2) The correct answer is: 8^{10}

This question tests your knowledge of exponent laws. First look to see whether your base number is the same on each part of the equation. (8 is the base number for each part of this equation.)

If the base number is the same, and the problem asks you to multiply, you add the exponents.

$8^7 \times 8^3 = 8^{(7+3)} = 8^{10}$

3) The correct answer is: 5^6

Look to see that your base number is the same on each part of the equation. (5 is the base number for this problem.)

If the base number is the same, and the problem asks you to divide, you subtract the exponents.

$5^8 \div 5^2 = 5^{8-2} = 5^6$

4) The correct answer is: $5^{\frac{1}{2}}$

Remember that $\sqrt{x} = x^{\frac{1}{2}}$

5) The correct answer is: $3\sqrt{7}$

In order to add square roots like this, you need to add the numbers in front of the square root sign.

$\sqrt{7} + 2\sqrt{7} =$
$1\sqrt{7} + 2\sqrt{7} =$
$3\sqrt{7}$

6) The correct answer is: $\sqrt{6}$

In order to multiply two square roots, multiply the numbers inside the square roots.

$2 \times 3 = 6$

Then put this result inside a square root symbol for your answer: $\sqrt{6}$

7) The correct answer is: $\sqrt{16}$

Multiply and put the result inside the square root symbol for your answer:

$$\sqrt{8} \times \sqrt{2} = \sqrt{16}$$

8) The correct answer is: 2

In equations that have both integers and square roots, your first step is to deal with the integer that is in front of the parentheses.

$5 + 5(3\sqrt{x} + 4) = 55$

$5 + 15\sqrt{x} + 20 = 55$

$25 + 15\sqrt{x} = 55$

$25 - 25 + 15\sqrt{x} = 55 - 25$

$15\sqrt{x} = 30$

Then divide.

$15\sqrt{x} = 30$

$(15\sqrt{x}) \div 15 = 30 \div 15$

$\sqrt{x} = 2$

9) The correct answer is: $5 = \log_2 32$

Logarithmic functions are just another way of expressing exponents. Remember that:

$y^x = Z$ is always the same as $x = \log_y Z$

10) The correct answer is: $1 \div x^7$

A negative exponent is always equal to 1 divided by the variable with a positive exponent.

Therefore, $x^{-7} = 1 \div x^7$

11) The correct answer is: $\dfrac{35x}{4}$

To solve this problem, multiply the numerator of the first fraction by the numerator of the second fraction to calculate the numerator of the new fraction. Then multiply the denominators in order to get the new denominator. Then simplify, if possible.

$$\frac{5x^3}{4} \times \frac{7}{x^2} = \frac{35x^3}{4x^2} = \frac{35x}{4}$$

12) The correct answer is: $18x^5$

Multiply the base numbers and add the exponents, being careful with the negatives.

$$\left(-3x\right)\left(-6x^4\right)=$$

$$-3x^1 \times -6^4 =$$

$$18x^5$$

13) The correct answer is: $\dfrac{x^2 + 2x}{x^2 + 9x + 20}$

Factor the numerators and denominators.

$$\frac{x^2 + 8x + 12}{x^2 + 8x + 16} \times \frac{x^2 + 4x}{x^2 + 11x + 30} =$$

$$\frac{(x+2)(x+6)}{(x+4)(x+4)} \times \frac{x(x+4)}{(x+5)(x+6)}$$

Then cancel out the common terms and re-simplify.

$$\frac{(x+2)(x+6)}{(x+4)(x+4)} \times \frac{x(x+4)}{(x+5)(x+6)} =$$

$$\frac{x(x+2)}{(x+4)(x+5)} =$$

$$\frac{x^2 + 2x}{x^2 + 9x + 20}$$

14) The correct answer is: $\dfrac{8x + 5}{x^3 + 2x^2 + x}$

39

Factor the denominators of each fraction in order to help you find the lowest common denominator (LCD).

$$\frac{3}{x^2 + 2x + 1} + \frac{5}{x^2 + x} =$$

$$\frac{3}{(x+1)(x+1)} + \frac{5}{x(x+1)} =$$

$$\frac{x}{x} \times \frac{3}{(x+1)(x+1)} + \frac{5}{x(x+1)} \times \frac{(x+1)}{(x+1)} =$$

$$\frac{3x}{x(x+1)(x+1)} + \frac{5x+5}{x(x+1)(x+1)} =$$

$$\frac{8x+5}{x(x+1)(x+1)}$$

Then re-simplify after you have determined the LCD.

$$\frac{8x+5}{x(x+1)(x+1)} =$$

$$\frac{8x+5}{x(x^2 + 2x + 1)}$$

$$\frac{8x+5}{x^3 + 2x^2 + x}$$

15) The correct answer is: −24

Eliminate the fraction by multiplying both sides of the equation by −8.

$$3 = -\frac{1}{8}x$$

$$3 \times -8 = -\frac{1}{8}x \times -8$$

$$-24 = x$$

16) The correct answer is: 10

Square both sides of the equation and then isolate x in order to solve the problem.

$$\sqrt{4x-4} = 6$$

$$\sqrt{4x-4}^2 = 6^2$$

$$4x - 4 = 36$$

$$4x - 4 + 4 = 36 + 4$$

$$4x = 40$$

$$x = 10$$

17) The correct answer is: $\dfrac{7x}{4}$

Invert and multiply by the second fraction.

$$\frac{7x+7}{x} \div \frac{4x+4}{x^2} =$$

$$\frac{7x+7}{x} \times \frac{x^2}{4x+4}$$

Factor and then cancel out as much as possible

$$\frac{7x+7}{x} \times \frac{x^2}{4x+4} =$$

$$\frac{7(x+1)}{x} \times \frac{x^2}{4(x+1)} =$$

$$\frac{7x^2}{4x}$$

Then simplify the resulting fraction in order to get your final result.

$$\frac{7x^2}{4x} = \frac{7x}{4}$$

18) The correct answer is: $7x^7$

This is another exponent problem in a slightly different form. Again, you have to remember the basic principles of factoring and of multiplying numbers that have exponents. Remember to multiply base numbers and add exponents.

$$49x^8 = 7x(\ )$$

$$7x \times 7x^7 = 49x^8$$

19) The correct answer is: $-x^8 + 11x^5$

Deal with the negative sign in front of the second set of parentheses. Then group like terms together in order to simplify.

$$(4x^8 + 5x^5 - 7) - (-6x^5 + 5x^8 - 7) =$$

$$4x^8 + 5x^5 - 7 + 6x^5 - 5x^8 + 7 =$$

$$4x^8 - 5x^8 + 5x^5 + 6x^5 - 7 + 7 =$$

$$-x^8 + 11x^5$$

20) The correct answer is: $6x$

Compare the denominator of the first fraction with the denominator of the second fraction and divide, if possible, in order to find the common factor: $9x^2 \div 3x = 3x$

Now multiply the numerator on the first fraction by this result in order to get the numerator of the second fraction: $2 \times 3x = 6x$

21) The correct answer is: $\dfrac{11x + 16}{x^2 + 2x}$

The LCD in this problem is $x^2 + 2x$. Remember to multiply the numerator and denominator by the same amounts when converting to the LCD.

$$\frac{8}{x} + \frac{3}{x+2} =$$

$$\frac{8}{x} \times \frac{x+2}{x+2} + \frac{3}{x+2} \times \frac{x}{x} =$$

$$\frac{8x+16}{x^2+2x} + \frac{3x}{x^2+2x} =$$

$$\frac{8x+16+3x}{x^2+2x} =$$

$$\frac{11x+16}{x^2+2x}$$

22) The correct answer is: $\dfrac{3B}{C}$

Isolate D by eliminating the fraction and dividing by C.

$$B = \frac{1}{3}CD$$

$$B \times 3 = \frac{1}{3} \times 3CD$$

$$3B = CD$$

$$3B \div C = CD \div C$$

$$\frac{3B}{C} = D$$

23) The correct answer is: $-{}^2/_3$ and -2

Factor the equation and then substitute 0 in each part of the factored equation to get your result.

$$6x^2 + 16x + 8 = 0$$

$$(3x + 2)(2x + 4) = 0$$

Now substitute 0 for *x* in the first pair of parentheses.

$(3 \times 0 + 2)(2x + 4) = 0$

$2(2x + 4) = 0$

$4x + 8 = 0$

$x = -2$

Then substitute 0 for *x* in the second pair of parentheses.

$(3x + 2)(2x + 4) = 0$

$(3x + 2)(2 \times 0 + 4) = 0$

$(3x + 2)4 = 0$

$12x + 8 = 0$

$12x + 8 - 8 = 0 - 8$

$12x = -8$

$x = -{}^{8}/_{12}$

$x = -{}^{2}/_{3}$

24) The correct answer is: x^{10}

$$\frac{x^2}{x^{-8}} = x^2 \div x^{-8} = x^{2--8} = x^{10}$$

25) The correct answer is: $\dfrac{XY}{W}$

Multiply each side of the equation by *Z*. Then divide by *W* in order to isolate *Z*.

$$W = \frac{XY}{Z}$$

$$W \times Z = \frac{XY}{Z} \times Z$$

$$WZ = XY$$

$$WZ \div W = XY \div W$$

$$Z = \frac{XY}{W}$$

26) The correct answer is: $\dfrac{14x - 20}{105x^2}$

You will know by now that you need to find the LCD and then perform the operation.

$$\frac{2}{15x} - \frac{4}{21x^2} =$$

$$\frac{2}{15x} \times \frac{7x}{7x} - \frac{4}{21x^2} \times \frac{5}{5} =$$

$$\frac{14x}{105x^2} - \frac{20}{105x^2} =$$

$$\frac{14x - 20}{105x^2}$$

27) The correct answer is: 17

Place the stated values into the equation and perform the operations in order to solve the problem.

$$A = \frac{1}{2}(B + C)d$$

$$120 = \frac{1}{2}(13 + C)8$$

$$120 \div 8 = \frac{1}{2}(13 + C)8 \div 8$$

$$15 = \frac{1}{2}(13 + C)$$

$$15 \times 2 = \frac{1}{2} \times 2(13 + C)$$

$$30 = 13 + C$$

$$17 = C$$

28) The correct answer is: $50a^2b^{12} - 40ab^8 - 100a^2b^5$

Step 1: Apply the distributive property of multiplication by multiplying the item in front of the opening parenthesis by each item inside the pair of parentheses.

Step 2: Add up the individual products in order to solve the problem.

$$10ab^5(5ab^7 - 4b^3 - 10a) =$$

$$(10ab^5 \times 5ab^7) - (10ab^5 \times 4b^3) - (10ab^5 \times 10a) =$$

$$50a^2b^{12} - 40ab^8 - 100a^2b^5$$

29) The correct answer is: −5

Assign a variable to the mystery number. In this case, we will call the number x. Then make an equation based on the information stated in the problem.

twice a number = 2x

8 less than the number = x − 8

the sum of twice a number and 8 less than the number = 2x + x − 8

the difference between −28 and the number = −28 − x

So the equation is: 2x + x − 8 = −28 − x

Finally, solve the equation for x.

2x + x − 8 = −28 − x
2x + x − 8 + 8 = −28 + 8 − x
2x + x = −20 − x
2x + x + x = −20 − x + x
4x = −20
x = −5

30) The correct answer is: $z + 2$

Remember to invert and multiply.

$$\frac{z^2 + 7z + 10}{z^2 + 13z + 40} \div \frac{z + 8}{z^2 + 16z + 64} =$$

$$\frac{z^2 + 7z + 10}{z^2 + 13z + 40} \times \frac{z^2 + 16z + 64}{z + 8}$$

Then factor and re-simplify, canceling out where needed.

$$\frac{z^2 + 7z + 10}{z^2 + 13z + 40} \times \frac{z^2 + 16z + 64}{z + 8} =$$

$$\frac{(z + 2)(z + 5)}{(z + 8)(z + 5)} \times \frac{(z + 8)(z + 8)}{z + 8} =$$

$$\frac{(z + 2)}{1} =$$

$$z + 2$$

31) The correct answer is: $x^2 + 1$

When you see fractions that have fractions within themselves, treat the denominator as the division sign, and then invert and multiply the fractions as usual.

$$\frac{x + \dfrac{1}{x}}{\dfrac{1}{x}} =$$

$$\left(x + \frac{1}{x} \right) \div \frac{1}{x} =$$

$$\left(x + \frac{1}{x} \right) \times x =$$

$$x^2 + \frac{x}{x} =$$

$$x^2 + 1$$

32) The correct answer is: 10

Eliminate the integer.

$$\frac{3a}{10} + 9 = 12$$

$$\frac{3a}{10} + 9 - 9 = 12 - 9$$

$$\frac{3a}{10} = 3$$

Then eliminate the fraction and isolate a in order to solve the problem.

$$\frac{3a}{10} = 3$$

$$\frac{3a}{10} \times 10 = 3 \times 10$$

$$3a = 30$$

$$a = 10$$

33) The correct answer is: $x = \sqrt{5}$

First you need to eliminate the denominator of the fraction.

$$\frac{18}{\sqrt{x^2 + 4}} = 6$$

$$\frac{18}{\sqrt{x^2 + 4}} \times (\sqrt{x^2 + 4}) = 6 \times (\sqrt{x^2 + 4})$$

$$18 = 6\sqrt{x^2 + 4}$$

Then eliminate the integer in front of the radical.

$$18 = 6\sqrt{x^2 + 4}$$

$$18 \div 6 = (6\sqrt{x^2 + 4}) \div 6$$

$$3 = \sqrt{x^2 + 4}$$

Then square both sides of the equation in order to solve the problem.

$$3 = \sqrt{x^2 + 4}$$

$$3^2 = (\sqrt{x^2 + 4})^2$$

$$9 = x^2 + 4$$

$$9 - 4 = x^2 + 4 - 4$$

$$5 = x^2$$

$$x = \sqrt{5}$$

34) The correct answer is: $\frac{4}{5}$

You have to find the cube roots of the numerator and denominator in order to eliminate the radical.

$$\sqrt[3]{\frac{64}{125}} = \sqrt[3]{\frac{4 \times 4 \times 4}{5 \times 5 \times 5}} = \frac{4}{5}$$

35) The correct answer is: 14

First you need to eliminate the fraction and simplify the result as far as possible. Then remove the common terms and integers in order to isolate a and solve the problem.

$$\frac{b^2 - ab + 24}{b - 12} = b - 2$$

$$\frac{b^2 - ab + 24}{b - 12} \times (b - 12) = (b - 2)(b - 12)$$

$b^2 - ab + 24 = (b - 2)(b - 12)$

$b^2 - ab + 24 = b^2 - 14b + 24$

$b^2 - b^2 - ab + 24 - 24 = b^2 - b^2 - 14b + 24 - 24$

$-ab = -14b$

$a = 14$

36) The correct answer is: $\dfrac{1}{25}$

Tip 1: When you see a fraction as an exponent, remember that you need to place the base number inside the radical sign. The denominator of the exponent is the nth root of the radical, and the numerator of the fraction becomes the new exponent. Here is an example: $x^{3/4} = (\sqrt[4]{x})^3$

Tip 2: When you see a negative exponent, you remove the negative sign on the exponent by expressing the number as a fraction, with 1 as the numerator. Here is an example: $x^{-6} = \dfrac{1}{x^6}$

So you need to combine these two principles in order to solve the problem.

$$125^{-2/3} = \dfrac{1}{125^{2/3}} = \dfrac{1}{\sqrt[3]{125}^2} = \dfrac{1}{(\sqrt[3]{5 \cdot 5 \cdot 5})^2} = \dfrac{1}{5^2} = \dfrac{1}{25}$$

37) The correct answer is: 9

Eliminate the fraction and the integer. Then eliminate the radical by squaring both sides of the equation. Finally, isolate x to solve the problem.

$$\dfrac{20}{\sqrt{x^2 + 7}} = 5$$

$$\dfrac{20}{\sqrt{x^2 + 7}} \times \sqrt{x^2 + 7} = 5 \times \sqrt{x^2 + 7}$$

$$20 = 5\sqrt{x^2 + 7}$$

$$20 \div 5 = (5\sqrt{x^2 + 7}) \div 5$$

$$4 = \sqrt{x^2 + 7}$$

$$4^2 = (\sqrt{x^2 + 7})^2$$

$$16 = x^2 + 7$$

$$16 - 7 = x^2 + 7 - 7$$

$$9 = x^2$$

Tip: Read these types of problems carefully. Sometimes they will ask you to solve for x^2 and other times they will ask you to solve for x.

38) The correct answer is: $\dfrac{4\sqrt{3}}{3}$

"Rationalize" means to remove the square root symbol by performing the necessary mathematical operations.

We remove the square root from the denominator as follows:

$$\sqrt{\dfrac{16}{3}} = \dfrac{\sqrt{16}}{\sqrt{3}} = \dfrac{\sqrt{4 \times 4}}{\sqrt{3}} = \dfrac{4}{\sqrt{3}} = \dfrac{4 \times \sqrt{3}}{\sqrt{3} \times \sqrt{3}} = \dfrac{4\sqrt{3}}{3}$$

39) The correct answer is: $106 - 19\sqrt{10}$

Tip 1: Don't panic when you see the radicals. This is just another type of FOIL problem.

Tip 2: When you multiply radicals, multiply the numbers in front of the radicals and then the numbers inside the radicals. Here is an example: $3\sqrt{3} \times 4\sqrt{2} = 12\sqrt{6}$

Now here is the solution to the problem.

$$(\sqrt{2} - 5\sqrt{5})(3\sqrt{2} - 4\sqrt{5}) =$$

$$(\sqrt{2} \times 3\sqrt{2}) + (\sqrt{2} \times -4\sqrt{5}) + (-5\sqrt{5} \times 3\sqrt{2}) + (-5\sqrt{5} \times -4\sqrt{5}) =$$

$$(3 \times 2) + (-4\sqrt{10}) + (-15\sqrt{10}) + (20 \times 5) =$$

$$6 - 4\sqrt{10} - 15\sqrt{10} + 100 = 106 - 19\sqrt{10}$$

40) The correct answer is: $4x^2y$

When the denominator of a fraction contains another fraction, treat the main fraction as the division sign. Then invert and multiply as usual.

$$\frac{4x}{\frac{1}{xy}} = 4x \div \frac{1}{xy} = 4x \times xy = 4x^2y$$

41) The correct answer is: 512

Here is some further practice with some concepts we have seen earlier. Remember that when you see a fraction as an exponent, you need to place the base number inside the radical sign. The denominator of the exponent is the nth root of the radical, and the numerator of the fraction becomes the new exponent. Here is an example: $x^{3/4} = (\sqrt[4]{x})^3$

You will need to simplify the radical as much as possible.

So for our problem: $64^{3/2} = \sqrt{64}^3 = (\sqrt{8 \times 8})^3 = 8^3 = 512$

42) The correct answer is: $\dfrac{10\sqrt{3} + 5\sqrt{5}}{6}$

Find the LCD and then perform the operations, including simplification of the radical, in order to solve the problem.

$$\frac{\sqrt{75}}{3} + \frac{5\sqrt{5}}{6} =$$

$$\frac{\sqrt{75}}{3} \times \frac{2}{2} + \frac{5\sqrt{5}}{6} =$$

$$\frac{2\sqrt{75}}{6} + \frac{5\sqrt{5}}{6} =$$

$$\frac{2\sqrt{75} + 5\sqrt{5}}{6} =$$

$$\frac{2\sqrt{25 \times 3} + 5\sqrt{5}}{6} =$$

$$\frac{2 \times 5\sqrt{3} + 5\sqrt{5}}{6} =$$

$$\frac{10\sqrt{3} + 5\sqrt{5}}{6}$$

43) The correct answer is: $2 + \dfrac{5\sqrt{5}}{9}$

Here it appears that we have a mixed number on the second fraction. However, don't let this confuse you. The basic concepts are the same as in the preceding problem.

$$\frac{\sqrt{36}}{3} + 5\frac{\sqrt{5}}{9} =$$

$$\frac{\sqrt{36}}{3} + \frac{5\sqrt{5}}{9} =$$

$$\frac{\sqrt{36}}{3} \times \frac{3}{3} + \frac{5\sqrt{5}}{9} =$$

$$\frac{3\sqrt{36}}{9} + \frac{5\sqrt{5}}{9} =$$

$$\frac{3 \times 6}{9} + \frac{5\sqrt{5}}{9} =$$

$$\frac{18}{9} + \frac{5\sqrt{5}}{9} =$$

$$\frac{18 + 5\sqrt{5}}{9} =$$

$$2 + \frac{5\sqrt{5}}{9}$$

44) The correct answer is: $3\sqrt{2} + 35\sqrt{3}$

Find the squared factors of the amounts inside the radical signs. Then simplify.

$$\sqrt{18} + 4\sqrt{75} + 5\sqrt{27} =$$

$$\sqrt{2 \times 9} + 4\sqrt{3 \times 25} + 5\sqrt{3 \times 9} =$$

$$3\sqrt{2} + (4 \times 5)\sqrt{3} + (5 \times 3)\sqrt{3} =$$

$$3\sqrt{2} + 20\sqrt{3} + 15\sqrt{3} =$$

$$3\sqrt{2} + 35\sqrt{3}$$

45) The correct answer is: $24x^4 + 18x^3 - 2x^2 - 24x - 40$

Use the distributive property of multiplication, group like terms together, and then simplify.

$(4x^2 + 3x + 5)(6x^2 - 8) =$

$(4x^2 \times 6x^2) + (3x \times 6x^2) + (5 \times 6x^2) + [(4x^2 \times -8) + (3x \times -8) + (5 \times -8)] =$

$24x^4 + 18x^3 + 30x^2 + (-32x^2 + -24x + -40) =$

$24x^4 + 18x^3 + 30x^2 - 32x^2 - 24x - 40 =$

$24x^4 + 18x^3 - 2x^2 - 24x - 40$

46) The correct answer is: $6xy(1 - 2x - 4xy)$

In order to factor an equation, you must figure out what terms are common to each term of the equation. Let's factor out xy.

$6xy - 12x^2y - 24y^2x^2 =$
$xy(6 - 12x - 24xy)$

Then think about integers. We can see that all of the terms inside the parentheses are divisible by 6. Now let's factor out the 6. In order to do this, we divide each term inside the parentheses by 6.

$xy(6 - 12x - 24xy) =$
$6xy(1 - 2x - 4xy)$

47) The correct answer is: $2x^6\sqrt{6}$

Tip: When the two radicals symbols are together like this, you need to multiply them.

$$\sqrt{4x^8}\sqrt{6x^4} =$$

$$\sqrt{4x^8} \times \sqrt{6x^4} =$$

$$\sqrt{24x^{12}} = \sqrt{4 \times 6} \times \sqrt{x^{12}} = 2\sqrt{6} \times x^{\frac{12}{2}} = 2x^6\sqrt{6}$$

48) The correct answer is: 3i

Note that it is not possible to find the square root of a negative number by using real numbers. Therefore, you will have to use imaginary numbers to solve this problem. Imaginary numbers are represented by the variable i.

So first determine what the square root of the number would be if the number were positive.

$$\sqrt{9} = 3$$

Now multiply that result by i.

$3 \times i = 3i$

49) The correct answer is: $\log_3 243 = 5$

$\log_y Z = x$ is always the same as $y^x = Z$

So $3^5 = 243$ is the same as $\log_3 243 = 5$

50) The correct answer is: (1, −3)

Plug in values for *x* and *y* to see if they work for both equations.

Answer choice (D) is the only answer that works for both equations.

If *x* = 1, then for the first equation:

$y = (-2 \times 1) - 1$
$y = -2 - 1$
$y = -3$

For the second equation:

$y = x - 4$
$-3 = x - 4$
$-3 + 4 = x - 4 + 4$
$1 = x$

51) The correct answer is: 12

Tip: When you see the sigma sign like this, you need to perform the operation at the right-hand side of the sigma sign. In this problem, we perform the operation for $x = 2$, $x = 3$ and $x = 4$ (because 4 is the number at the top). Then we add these individual products together to get the final result.

For $x = 2$: $x + 1 = 2 + 1 = 3$

For $x = 3$: $x + 1 = 3 + 1 = 4$

For $x = 4$: $x + 1 = 4 + 1 = 5$

$3 + 4 + 5 = 12$

52) The correct answer is: $5a^2$

Hopefully you will be comfortable with this type of problem at this point.

Treat the main fraction as division by inverting and multiplying. Then simplify.

$$\frac{a^3/ab}{b/5b^2} = \left. a^3 \middle/ ab \right. \div \left. b \middle/ 5b^2 \right. = \left. a^3 \middle/ ab \right. \times \left. 5b^2 \middle/ b \right. = \left. 5a^3 b^2 \middle/ ab^2 \right. = \left. ab^2(5a^2) \middle/ ab^2 \right. = 5a^2$$

53) The correct answer is: 36

Look at the relationship between X and Y in order to solve the problem.

In each case, we can see that $Y = X^2$

So if $X = 6$, $Y = 36$

54) The correct answer is: x^6/y^9

Tip: When raising a power to a power, you have to multiply the exponent outside of the parentheses by the exponents inside the parentheses.

$(x^2 \div y^3)^3 =$

$x^6 \div y^9 =$

x^6/y^9

55) The correct answer is: 2^6

$2^4 \times 2^2 = 2^{(4 + 2)} = 2^6$

56) The correct answer is: $-3x^4 + 7x^3 + 17x^2 - 35x - 10$

Change the positions of the sets of parentheses.

$(-3x^2 + 7x + 2)(x^2 - 5) =$

$(x^2 - 5)(-3x^2 + 7x + 2)$

Multiply the first term from the first set of parentheses by all of the terms in the second set of parentheses. Then multiply the second term from the first set of parentheses by all of the terms in the second set of parentheses.

$(x^2 - 5)(-3x^2 + 7x + 2) =$

$(x^2 \times -3x^2) + (x^2 \times 7x) + (x^2 \times 2) + (-5 \times -3x^2) + (-5 \times 7x) + (-5 \times 2) =$

$-3x^4 + 7x^3 + 2x^2 + 15x^2 - 35x - 10$

Then simplify.

$-3x^4 + 7x^3 + 2x^2 + 15x^2 - 35x - 10 =$

$-3x^4 + 7x^3 + 17x^2 - 35x - 10$

57) The correct answer is: A^{12}

When taking an exponential number to another exponent, you have to multiply the exponents.

$(A^5 \div A^2)^4 =$

$(A^{5-2})^4 =$

$(A^3)^4 =$

A^{12}

58) The correct answer is: 0.25

We have the special operation defined as: $(x \, Д \, y) = (2x \div 4y)$.

First of all, look at the relationship between the left-hand side and the right-hand side of this equation in order to determine which operations you need to perform on any new equation containing the operation Д and variables x and y.

In other words, in any new equation:

Operation Д is division.
The number or variable immediately after the opening parenthesis is multiplied by 2.
The number or variable immediately before the closing parenthesis is multiplied by 4.

So the equation $(8\ Д\ y) = 16$ becomes $(2 \times 8) \div (4 \times y) = 16$

Now solve for $(2 \times 8) \div (4 \times y) = 16$

$(2 \times 8) \div (4 \times y) = 16$

$16 \div 4y = 16$

$16 = 16 \times 4y$

$16 = 64y$

$y = 0.25$

59) The correct answer is: 25

First solve for the function in the inner–most set of parentheses, in this case $f_1(x)$.

For $x = 2$, $f_1(2) = 5$

Then take this new value to solve for $f_2(x)$

For $x = 5$, $f_2(x) = 25$

60) The correct answer is: C

Two whole numbers that are greater than 1 will always result in a greater number when they are multiplied by each other, rather than when those numbers are divided by each other or subtracted from each other.

Practice Problems – Geometry and Measurement:

1) The graph of $y = 8 \div (x - 4)$ is shown below:

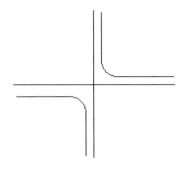

Which of the following is the best representation of $8 \div | (x - 4) | $?

A.

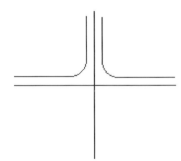

B.

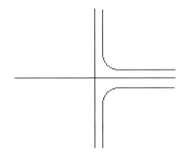

C.

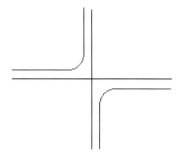

D.

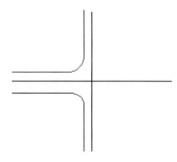

2) Which of the following is the graph of the solution set of $-3x > 6$?

A.

B.

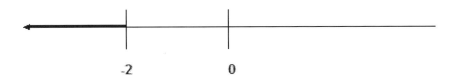

-2   0

C.

-4   0   4

D.

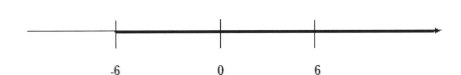

-6   0   6

3) If a circle has a diameter of 18, what is the circumference of the circle?

4) If circle A has a radius of 0.4 and circle B has a radius of 0.2, what is the difference in area between the two circles?

5) If a circle A has a radius of 4, what is the circumference of the circle?

6) If a circle has a radius of 6, what is the area of the circle?

7) Find the coordinates (x, y) of the midpoint of the line segment on a graph that connects these points: $(-5, 3)$ and $(3, -5)$.

8) State the x and y intercepts that fall on the straight line represented by the following equation:

$y = x + 6$

9) Consider a two-dimensional linear graph where $x = 3$ and $y = 14$. The line crosses the y axis at 5. What is the slope of this line?

10) What ordered pair is a solution to the following system of equations?

$x + y = 11$
$xy = 24$

11) Write the slope-intercept equation for the following coordinates: (3,0) and (8,2)

12) Calculate the slope and the y intercept: $3x + 5y = 24$

13) Consider a right-angled triangle, where side M and side N form the right angle, and side L is the hypotenuse. If M = 3 and N = 2, what is the length of side L?

14) Find the volume of a cylinder whose height is 18 and whose radius is 4. Use 3.14 for π.

15) Prepare the slope-intercept formula, using the data from the following table:

x	0	4	8
y	5	1	–3

16) Find the x and y intercepts of the following equation: $4x^2 + 9y^2 = 36$

17) Find the midpoint between the following coordinates: (2, 2) and (4, –6)

18) In the standard (x,y) plane, what is the distance between (3,0) and (6,4)?

19) Give the slope-intercept formula that defines a line which is perpendicular to the line given by the formula: $y = \frac{1}{2}x + 5$

20) In the standard (x,y) plane, what is the distance between $(3\sqrt{5},0)$ and $(6\sqrt{5},4)$?

21) What equation defines a line that is parallel to the line given by the following equation:

$y = -0.5x + 5$?

22) Find the area of the right triangle whose base is 2 and height is 5.

23) Find the volume of a cone which has a radius of 3 and a height of 4.

24) Consider a right–angled triangle, where side A and side B form the right angle, and side C is the hypotenuse. If A = 5 and B = 3, what is the length of side C?

25) Consider the vertex of an angle at the center of a circle. If the diameter of the circle is 2, and if the angle measures 90 degrees, what is the arc length relating to the angle?

26) Pat wants to put wooden trim around the floor of her family room. Each piece of wood is 1 foot in length. The room is rectangular and is 12 feet wide and 10 feet long. How many pieces of wood does Pat need for the entire perimeter of the room?

27) The Johnson's have decided to remodel their upstairs. They currently have 4 rooms upstairs that measure 10 feet by 10 feet each. When they remodel, they will make one large room that will be 20 feet by 10 feet and two small rooms that will each be 10 feet by 8 feet. The remaining space is to be allocated to a new bathroom. What are the dimensions of the new bathroom?

28) In the figure below, the larger circle is centered at B and is internally tangent to the smaller circle, which is centered at A. The length of line segment AB, which is the radius of the smaller circle, is 3 units, and the radius of the smaller circle passes through the center of the larger circle. If the area of the smaller circle is removed from the larger circle, what is the remaining area of the larger circle?

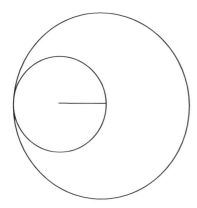

29) The perimeter of the square shown below is 24 units. What is the length of line segment AB?

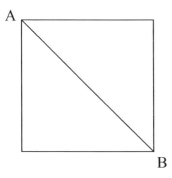

30) In the figure below, *x* and *y* are parallel lines, and line *z* is a transversal crossing both *x* and *y*. Which three angles are equal in measure? (There are two possible answers.)

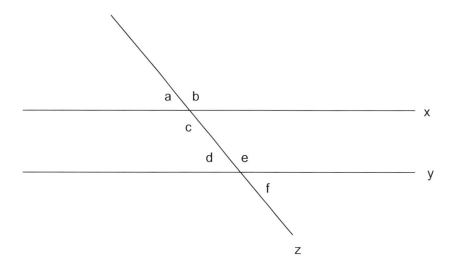

31) The central angle in the circle below measures 45° and is subtended by an arc which is 4π centimeters in length. How many centimeters long is the radius of this circle?

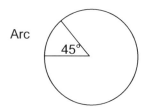

32) In the figure below, XY and WZ are parallel, and lengths are provided in units. What is the area of trapezoid WXYZ in square units?

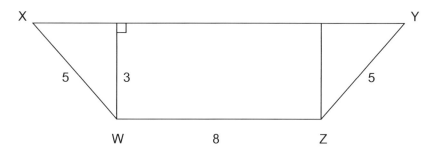

33) In the figure below, the lengths of KL, LM, and KN are provided in units. What is the area of triangle NLM in square units?

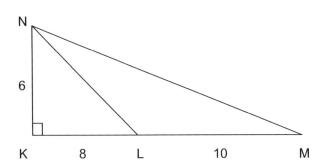

N

6

K   8   L   10   M

34) ∠XYZ is an isosceles triangle, where XY is equal to YZ. Angle Y is 30° and points W, X, and Z are co–linear. What is the measurement of ∠WXY?

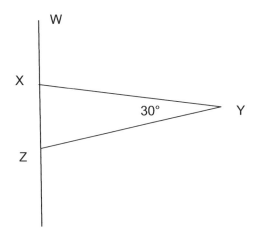

W

X

30°   Y

Z

35) In the right triangle below, the length of AC is 5 units and the length of BC is 4 units. What is the tangent of ∠A ?

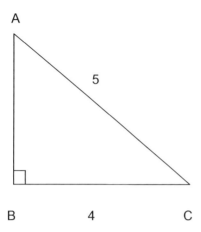

36) In the right angle in the figure below, the length of XZ is 10 units, sin 40° = 0.643, cos 40° = 0.776, and tan 40° = 0.839. Approximately how many units long is XY?

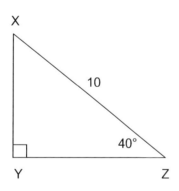

37) An arc length of θ on a circle of radius one subtends an angle of how many radians at the center of the circle?

38) If the radius of a circle is 1, what equation can be used to find the radians in 90°?

39) The perimeter of a rectangle is 64 meters. If the width were increased by 2 meters and the length were increased by 3 meters, what is the perimeter of the new rectangle?

40) Find the volume of a box which is 14 inches high, 8 inches wide, and 10 inches long.

Solutions – Geometry and Measurement:

1) The correct answer is: A

We know from the original graph in the question that when x is a positive number, then y will also be positive. This is represented by the curve in the upper right–hand quadrant of the graph.

We also know from the original graph in the question that when x is negative, y will also be negative. This is represented by the curve in the lower left–hand quadrant of the graph.

If we add the absolute value symbols to the problem, then $|(x-4)|$ will always result in a positive value for y. Therefore, even when x is negative, y will be positive. So the curve originally represented in the lower left–hand quadrant of the graph must be shift into the upper left–hand quadrant.

2) The correct answer is: B

Isolate the unknown variable in order to solve the problem:

$-3x > 6$
$-3x \div 3 > 6 \div 3$
$-x > 2$

If the isolated variable is negative as in this problem, you need to reverse the greater than symbol, in order to make it the less than symbol.

$-x > 2$
$x < -2$

This is represented by line B.

3) The correct answer is: 18π

Circumference = π × diameter

4) The correct answer is: 0.12π

The area of a circle is always: π times the radius squared.

Therefore, the area of circle A is: $0.4^2\pi = 0.16\pi$
The area of circle B is: $0.2^2\pi = 0.04\pi$

To calculate the difference in area between the two circles, we then subtract.

$0.16\pi - 0.04\pi = 0.12\pi$

5) The correct answer is: 8π

rence of a circle is always calculated by using this formula.

iameter

(The diameter of a circle is always equal to the radius times 2.)

So the diameter for this circle is 4 × 2 = 8. Therefore, the circumference is 8π.

6) The correct answer is: 12π

The area of a circle is always: $\pi \times \text{radius}^2$

The radius of this circle is 6

Therefore, the circumference is 36π.

7) The correct answer is: (−1, −1)

In order to find midpoints on a line, you need to use the following formula:

For two points on a graph (x_1, y_1) and (x_2, y_2) , the midpoint is:

$(x_1 + x_2) \div 2$, $(y_1 + y_2) \div 2$

Now calculate for x and y.

$(−5 + 3) \div 2 = \text{midpoint } x$, $(3 + − 5) \div 2 = \text{midpoint } y$

$−2 \div 2 = \text{midpoint } x$, $−2 \div 2 = \text{midpoint } y$

$−1 = \text{midpoint } x$, $−1 = \text{midpoint } y$

8) The correct answer is: (−6, 0) and (0, 6)

To solve problems like this one, begin by substituting 0 for x.

$y = x + 6$
$y = 0 + 6$
$y = 6$

Therefore, the coordinates (0, 6) represent the y intercept.

Now substitute 0 for y.

$y = x + 6$
$0 = x + 6$
$0 − 6 = x + 6 − 6$
$−6 = x$

So the coordinates (–6, 0) represent the *x* intercept.

9) The correct answer is: 3

In order to calculate the slope of a line, you need this formula:

y = *mx* + *b*

NOTE: *m* is the slope and *b* is the *y* intercept (the point at which the line crosses the *y* axis).

Now solve for the numbers given in the problem.

14 = *m*3 + 5
14 – 5 = *m*3 + 5 – 5
9 = *m*3
9 ÷ 3 = *m*
3 = *m*

10) The correct answer is: (3, 8)

For questions on systems of equations like this one, you should look at the multiplication equation first. Ask yourself, what are the factors of 24?

We know that 24 is the product of the following:

1 × 24 = 24
2 × 12 = 24
3 × 8 = 24
4 × 6 = 24

Now add each of the two factors together to solve the first equation.

1 + 24 = 25

2 + 12 = 14

3 + 8 = 11

4 + 6 = 10

(3, 8) solves both equations. Therefore, it is the correct answer.

11) The correct answer is: $y = \frac{2}{5}x - \frac{6}{5}$

Find the slope, represented by variable *m*, by putting the stated values into the slope formula.

Slope formula: $\dfrac{y_2 - y_1}{x_2 - x_1} = m$

$\dfrac{2-0}{8-3} = \dfrac{2}{5}$

Then calculate the *y* intercept, represented by variable *b*, by putting the values for *x*, *y*, and *m* into the slope-intercept formula.

$y = mx - b$

$0 = (^2/_5 \times 3) - b$

$^6/_5 = b$

Finally, express as the slope-intercept equation, using variables *x* and *y*.

$y = {}^2/_5x - {}^6/_5$

12) The correct answer is: $b = {}^{24}/_5$ and $m = -{}^3/_5$

Plug in 0 for *x* in order to calculate *b*, the *y* intercept.

$3x + 5y = 24$

$3 \times 0 + 5y = 24$

$5y = 24$

$y = {}^{24}/_5$

(0, $^{24}/_5$) are the coordinates for the *y* intercept.

Now put in 0 for *y* in order to calculate *x*.

$3x + 5y = 24$

$3x + 5 \times 0 = 24$

$3x = 24$

$x = 8$

(8, 0) are the coordinates for the *x* intercept.

Next use the slope formula to calculate the slope. Remember to simplify the fraction as much as possible.

$$\frac{y_2 - y_1}{x_2 - x_1} = m$$

$$\frac{0 - \frac{24}{5}}{8 - 0} = m$$

$$\frac{-\frac{24}{5}}{8} = m$$

$$-\frac{24}{5} \div 8 = m$$

$$-\frac{24}{5} \times \frac{1}{8} = m$$

$$-\frac{24}{40} = m$$

$$-\frac{3 \times 8}{5 \times 8} = m$$

$$-\frac{3}{5} = m$$

13) The correct answer is: $\sqrt{13}$

The length of the hypotenuse is always the square root of the sum of the squares of the other two sides of the triangle.

hypotenuse length L = $\sqrt{M^2 + N^2}$

Now put in the values for the above problem.

L = $\sqrt{3^2 + 2^2}$
L = $\sqrt{9 + 4}$
L = $\sqrt{13}$

14) The correct answer is: 904.32

The formula for the volume (V) of a cylinder is: $V = \pi r^2 h$

71

In other words, to calculate the volume of a cylinder you take π times the radius squared times the height.

Place the stated values into the equation in order to solve the problem.

$V = \pi r^2 h$

$V = 3.14 \times 4^2 \times 18$

$V = 3.14 \times 16 \times 18$

$V = 904.32$

15) The correct answer is: $y = -x + 5$

First you need to calculate slope (which is variable m in the slope-intercept equation) using the slope formula: $\dfrac{y_2 - y_1}{x_2 - x_1}$

Substitute the values for x and y from the table in order to calculate the slope.

$$\dfrac{y_2 - y_1}{x_2 - x_1} =$$

$$\dfrac{1 - 5}{4 - 0} =$$

$$\dfrac{-4}{4} = -1$$

We know from the information provided in the table that the y intercept (which is variable b in the slope-intercept equation) is 5 because of the coordinates (0, 5).

So we place these values into the slope-intercept formula in order to solve the problem.

$y = mx + b$

$y = -1x + 5$

$y = -x + 5$

16) The correct answer is: (3, 0) and (0, 2)

Remember that for questions about x and y intercepts, you need to substitute 0 for x and y to solve the problem.

Solution for *y* intercept:

$4x^2 + 9y^2 = 36$
$4(0^2) + 9y^2 = 36$
$0 + 9y^2 = 36$
$9y^2 \div 9 = 36 \div 9$
$y^2 = 4$
$y = 2$

So the *y* intercept is (0, 2)

Solution for *x* intercept:

$4x^2 + 9y^2 = 36$
$4x^2 + 9(0^2) = 36$
$4x^2 + 0 = 36$
$4x^2 \div 4 = 36 \div 4$
$x^2 = 9$
$x = 3$

So the *x* intercept is (3, 0)

17) The correct answer is: (3, –2)

For two points on a graph (x_1, y_1) and (x_2, y_2), the midpoint is: $(x_1 + x_2) \div 2$, $(y_1 + y_2) \div 2$

Now calculate for *x* and *y*.

$(2 + 4) \div 2$ = midpoint *x*, $(2 - 6) \div 2$ = midpoint *y*

$6 \div 2$ = midpoint *x*, $-4 \div 2$ = midpoint *y*

3 = midpoint *x*, –2 = midpoint *y*

18) The correct answer is: 5

Tip: To solve this problem, you need the distance formula.

$$d = \sqrt{(x_2 - x_1)^2 + (y_2 - y_1)^2}$$

$$d = \sqrt{(6-3)^2 + (4-0)^2}$$

$$d = \sqrt{3^2 + 16}$$

$$d = \sqrt{9 + 16}$$

$$d = \sqrt{25}$$

$$d = 5$$

19) The correct answer is: $y = -2x + 5$

Tip: Two lines are perpendicular if the product of their slopes is equal to –1.

Step 1: Calculate the slope. We can see that the slope of the line stated in the problem is ½. Because the lines are perpendicular, we calculate the slope of the new line with this formula: ½ × m = –1

So the slope of the perpendicular line is –2.

Step 2: To solve the problem, put the slope that you calculated in step 1 into the formula given in the problem.

For the given line: $y = \dfrac{1}{2}x + 5$

For the perpendicular line: $y = -2x + 5$

20) The correct answer is: $\sqrt{61}$

You need the distance formula again.

$$d = \sqrt{(x_2 - x_1)^2 + (y_2 - y_1)^2}$$

$$d = \sqrt{(6\sqrt{5} - 3\sqrt{5})^2 + (4 - 0)^2}$$

$$d = \sqrt{(3\sqrt{5})^2 + 16}$$

$$d = \sqrt{(9 \times 5) + 16}$$

$$d = \sqrt{45 + 16}$$

$$d = \sqrt{61}$$

21) The correct answer is: $y = -0.5x + b$

Tip 1: If two lines are parallel, they will have the same slope. So we can use the same value for *m* into both equations.

Tip 2: Note that the parallel lines will have a different *y* intercept.

22) The correct answer is: 5

To solve this problem, you need the following equation:

Triangle area = (base × height) ÷ 2

Now substitute the amounts for base and height.

area = (2 × 5) ÷ 2 =
10 ÷ 2 =
5

23) The correct answer is: 12π

To find the volume of a cone, you need this formula:

Cone volume = (π × radius^2 × height) ÷ 3

Now substitute the values for base and height.

volume = ($\pi 3^2$ × 4) ÷ 3 =
($\pi 9$ × 4) ÷ 3 =
$\pi 36$ ÷ 3 =
12π

24) The correct answer is: $\sqrt{34}$

hypotenuse length C = $\sqrt{A^2 + B^2}$

Now put in the values for the above problem.

C = $\sqrt{A^2 + B^2}$
C = $\sqrt{5^2 + 3^2}$
C = $\sqrt{25 + 9}$
C = $\sqrt{34}$

25) The correct answer is: π/2

To solve this problem, you need these three principles:
(1) Arc length is the distance on the outside (or partial circumference) of a circle.
(2) The circumference of a circle is always π times the diameter.
(3) There are 360 degrees in a circle.

The angle in this problem is 90 degrees.

360 ÷ 90 = 4; In other words, we are dealing with the circumference of 1/4 of the circle.
Given that the circumference of this circle is 2π, and we are dealing only with 1/4 of the circle, then the arc length for this angle is:

2π ÷ 4 = π/2

26) The correct answer is: 44

Remember that the perimeter is the measurement along the outside edges of the rectangle or other area. If the room is 12 feet by ten feet, we need 12 feet × 2 to finish the long sides of the room and 10 feet × 2 to finish the shorter sides of the room.

(12 × 2) + (10 × 2) = 44

27) The correct answer is: 10 feet by 4 feet

First we have to calculate the total square footage available. If there are 4 rooms which are 10 by 10 each, we have this equation:

4 × (10 × 10) = 400 square feet in total

Now calculate the square footage of the new rooms.

20 × 10 = 200
2 rooms × (10 × 8) = 160
200 + 160 = 360 total square feet for the new rooms

So the remaining square footage for the bathroom is calculated by taking the total minus the square footage of the new rooms. 400 − 360 = 40 square feet

Since each existing room is 10 feet long, we know that the new bathroom also needs to be 10 feet long in order to fit in. So the new bathroom is 10 feet by 4 feet.

28) The correct answer is: 27π

Circle area: $\pi \times r^2$

Therefore, the area of circle A is: $3^2\pi = 9\pi$

Since the circles are internally tangent, the radius of circle B is calculated by taking the radius of circle A times 2. Therefore, the radius of circle B is $3 \times 2 = 6$

The area of circle B is: $6^2 \pi = 36\pi$

To calculate the remaining area of circle B, we subtract as follows:

$36\pi - 9\pi = 27\pi$

29) The correct answer is: $\sqrt{72}$

Remember that the perimeter is the measurement along the outside edge of a geometrical figure. Since the figure in this problem is a square, we know that the four sides are equal in length.

To find the length of one side, we therefore divide the perimeter by four: $24 \div 4 = 6$

Now we use the Pythagorean theorem to find the length of line segment AB.

Remember the Pythagorean theorem states that the length of the hypotenuse is equal to the square root of the sum of the squares of the two other sides. The hypotenuse is the part of a triangle that is opposite to the right angle, in this case AB is the hypotenuse.

So the hypotenuse length is the square root of $6^2 + 6^2$.

$6^2 + 6^2 = 36 + 36 = 72$

So the answer is $\sqrt{72}$

30) The correct answers are: $\angle$a, $\angle$d, and $\angle$f are equal and $\angle$b, $\angle$c, and $\angle$e are also equal.

In problems like this, remember that parallel angles will be equal. So, for example, angles a and d are equal, and angles b and e are equal. Also remember that adjacent angles will be equal when bisected by two parallel lines, as with lines x and y in this problem.

Angles b and c are adjacent, and angles d and f are also adjacent. So $\angle$a, $\angle$d, and $\angle$f are equal and $\angle$b, $\angle$c, and $\angle$e are also equal.

31) The correct answer is: 16

Remember that circumference = $\pi \times$ radius $\times$ 2. The angle given in the problem is 45°. If we divide the total 360° in the circle by the 45° angle, we have: $360 \div 45 = 8$

So there are 8 such arcs along this circle. We then have to multiply the number of arcs by the length of each arc to get the circumference of the circle: $8 \times 4\pi = 32\pi$ (circumference)

Then use the formula for the circumference of the circle.

$32\pi = \pi \times 2 \times$ radius
$32\pi \div 2 = \pi \times 2 \times$ radius $\div 2$
$16\pi = \pi \times$ radius
$16 =$ radius

32) The correct answer is: 36

First calculate the area of the central rectangle. Remember that the area of a rectangle is length times height: $8 \times 3 = 24$

Using the Pythagorean theorem, we know that the base of each triangle is 4:

$5^2 = 3^2 +$ base^2
$25 = 9 +$ base^2
$25 - 9 = 9 - 9 +$ base^2
$16 =$ base^2
$4 =$ base

Then calculate the area of each of the triangles on each side of the central rectangle. Remember that the area of a triangle is base times height divided by 2: $(4 \times 3) \div 2 = 6$

So the total area is the area of the main rectangle plus the area of each of the two triangles:

$24 + 6 + 6 = 36$

33) The correct answer is: 30

Remember that the area of a triangle is base times height divided by 2. First calculate the area of triangle NKM: $6 \times (8 + 10) \div 2 = 54$

Then calculate the area of the area of triangle NKL: $(6 \times 8) \div 2 = 24$

The remaining triangle NLM is then calculated by subtracting the area of triangle NKL from triangle NKM: $54 - 24 = 30$

34) The correct answer is: 105°

We know that any straight line is 180°. We also know that the sum of the degrees of the three angles of any triangle is also 180°. The sum of angles X, Y, and Z = 180, so the sum of angle X and angle Z equals $180° - 30° = 150°$.

Because the triangle is isosceles, angle X and angle Z are equivalent, so we can divide the remaining degrees by 2 as follows: $150° \div 2 = 75°$. In other words, angle X and angle Z are each 75°.

Then we need to subtract the degree of the angle $\angle$XYZ from 180° to get the measurement of $\angle$WXY: $180° - 75° = 105°$

35) The correct answer is: 4/3

Using the Pythagorean theorem, we know that:

$AB^2 + BC^2 = AC^2$
$AB^2 + 4^2 = 5^2$
$AB^2 + 16 = 25$
$AB^2 + 16 - 16 = 25 - 16$
$AB^2 = 9$
$AB = 3$

In this problem, the tangent of angle A is calculated by dividing BC by AB.

So the correct answer is 4 ÷ 3 = 4/3

36) The correct answer is: 6.43

The sin of angle Z is calculated by dividing XY by XZ.

sin z = XY/XZ
sin z = XY/10

Since angle Z is 40 degrees, we can substitute values as follows:

sin z = XY/10
0.643 = XY/10
0.643 × 10 = XY/10 × 10
0.643 × 10 = XY
6.43 = XY

37) The correct answer is: θ

If the radius is 1, the radians will be equal to the arc length. So the correct answer is θ.

38) The correct answer is: π ÷ 2 × radians = 90°

The radian is the angle subtended at the center of a circle by an arc that is equal in length to the radius of the circle.

Therefore, the radian is equal to 180 ÷ π , which is approximately 57.2958 degrees.

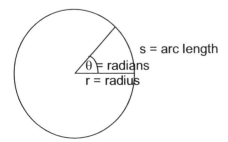
s = arc length
θ = radians
r = radius

The figure illustrates the calculation of radians. Remember this formula: $\theta = s \div r$

θ = the radians of the subtended angle
s = arc length
r = radius

Also remember these useful equations:

$\pi \div 6 \times$ radians = 30°
$\pi \div 4 \times$ radians = 45°
$\pi \div 2 \times$ radians = 90°
$\pi \times$ radians = 180°
$\pi \times 2 \times$ radians = 360°

Since this problem contains a 90 degree angle, the answer is the above equation for 90 degrees:

$\pi \div 2 \times$ radians = 90°

39) The correct answer is: 74 meters

Set up equations for the areas of the rectangles both before and after the change, using W for the width and L for the length. Then isolate variable W for the width. Finally, solve by expressing variable W in terms of L.

BEFORE:

2L + 2W = 64
2W = 64 − 2L
W = 32 − L

AFTER:

? = 2(L + 3) + 2(W + 2)
? = 2(L + 3) + 2(32 − L + 2)
? = (2L + 6) + 2(34 − L)
? = 2L + 6 + 68 − 2L
? = 6 + 68
? = 74

40) The correct answer is: 1120 cubic inches

To find the volume of a box, you need this formula: box volume = (length × width × height)

Now substitute the values for length, width, and height.

volume = (14 × 10 × 8) =
(14 × 80) =
1120

Practice Problems – Data Analysis, Statistics, and Probability:

1) Which age group, male or female, had the highest number of deaths from all three diseases (cancer, diabetes, and HIV in total)?

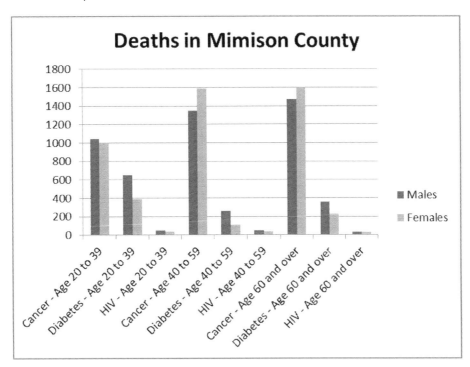

2) Which source provides the greatest amount of funding for the combined total of all three of the above types of costs?

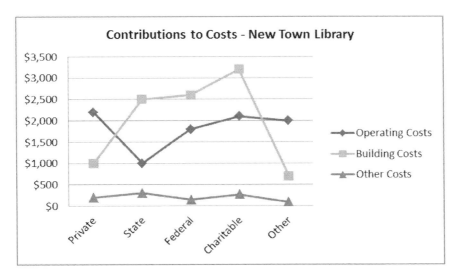

3) According to the graph, which area of the college has the highest percentage of use in total?

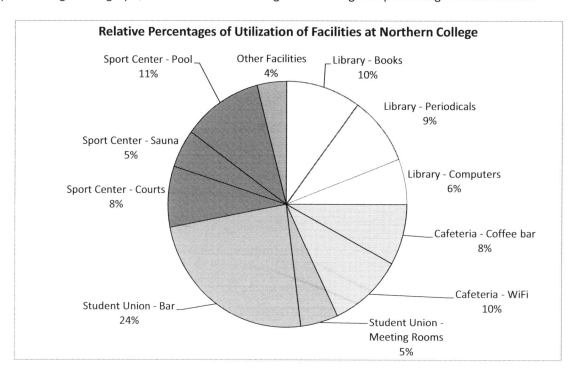

Relative Percentages of Utilization of Facilities at Northern College

- Sport Center - Pool 11%
- Other Facilities 4%
- Library - Books 10%
- Library - Periodicals 9%
- Sport Center - Sauna 5%
- Library - Computers 6%
- Sport Center - Courts 8%
- Cafeteria - Coffee bar 8%
- Cafeteria - WiFi 10%
- Student Union - Bar 24%
- Student Union - Meeting Rooms 5%

4) The table below shows information on vehicle ownership by different types of households in Mariposa County. How many retired couples own two or more vehicles?

Household type	Percentage of households of this type which own 2 or more vehicles (and total number of households)
single person	17% (59,000)
pre-retirement age couple, no children	54% (234,000)
pre-retirement age couple with children	78% (378,000)
single parent with children	23% (117,000)
retired couple	4% (56,000)
All households	55% (844,000)

5) 120 students took a math test. The mean score for the 60 female students was 95, while the mean score for the 60 male students was 90. What is the mean test score for all 120 students in the class?

6) Carmen wanted to find the mean of the five tests she has taken this semester. However, she erroneously divided the total points from the five tests by 4, which gave her a result of 90. What is the correct mean of her five tests?

7) In an athletic competition, the maximum possible amount of points was 25 points per participant. There were seven participants in the competition, and their scores were as follows: 2, 25, 23, 8, 21, 17, and 24. What was the median score?

8) An insurance appraiser assigns a number from 1 to 10 to indicate the level of damage to vehicles that have been in accidents. During one week, he appraises eight cars and assigns the following values to the damages: 2, 5, 6, 8, 7, 10. What was the median value?

9) An electricity company measures the energy consumption for each home in kilowatt hours. During July, one neighborhood had these levels of consumption: 1050, 201, 1500, 700, 1242, 1500, 1354, 289, 957. What is the mode of the level of energy consumption for this neighborhood for July?

10) The electricity company mentioned in the problem above measures the energy consumption for each home in kilowatt hours for August. In August, the neighborhood had these levels of consumption: 1080, 289, 1582, 739, 1080, 1582, 1504, 313, 969. What is the mode of the level of consumption for August?

11) The electricity company then measures the energy consumption for September. The levels of consumption are: 999, 305, 1602, 801, 987, 1408, 1654, 401, 1040. What is the mode for September?

12) Ten people in a support group are trying to lose weight. So far, the weight loss in pounds for each of the members of the group is as follows: 15, 8, 7, 3, 21, 24, 17, 14, 18, 20. What is the range of the amount of weight loss for the group?

13) Looking at our ten group members from the question above, what is the variance? Remember that the weight loss in pounds for each of the members of the group was as follows: 15, 8, 7, 3, 21, 24, 17, 14, 18, 20.

14) Now calculate the standard deviation for the weight loss group in the previous question.

15) How many members in the weight loss group are within one standard deviation of the mean?

16) The students in an English class received these grades on the mid-term exam: 96, 99, 97, 98, 64, 59, 83, 79, 67, 44, 72, and 57. What is the variance of the exam scores?

17) What is the standard deviation for the grades in the previous question?

18) A group of families had the following household incomes on their tax returns: $65000, $52000, $125000, $89000, $36000, $84000, $31000, $135000, $74000, and $87000. What is the range?

19) Return on investment (ROI) percentages are provided for seven companies. The ROI will be negative if the company operated at a loss, but the ROI will be a positive value if the company operated at a profit. The ROI's for the seven companies were: –2%, 5%, 7.5%, 14%, 17%, 1.3%, –3%. Find the median.

20) Find the mean ROI from the data provided in the previous problem.

21) Here are the prices of five used cars of a particular make and model:

$5,250
$5,299
$5,275
$5,300
$5,295

Calculate the variance in the five prices.

22) Now find the standard deviation for the prices of the five used cars.

23) How many cars are within one standard deviation of the mean?

24) 5 out of 50 students had test scores greater than 85. What score would a student need to achieve in order to be in the 90% percentile?

25) Which of these numbers cannot be a probability? (There is more than one answer.)

A. –0.02
B. 0
C. 1.002
D. 1

26) A jar contains 4 red marbles, 6 green marbles, and 10 white marbles. If a marble is drawn from the jar at random, what is the probability that this marble is white?

27) A magician has a bag of colored scarves for a magic trick that he performs. The bag contains 3 blue scarves, 1 red scarf, 5 green scarves, and 2 orange scarves. If the magician removes scarves at random and the first scarf he removes is red, what is the probability that the next scarf will be orange?

28) A card is drawn at random from a deck of cards. Find the probability of getting the ace of spades.

29) A card is drawn at random from a deck of cards. Find the probability of getting a king, queen, or jack.

30) A pair of dice is tossed. What is the probability that a sum greater than 9 will be obtained?

31) A pair of dice is tossed. What is the probability that a number less than 4 will be obtained?

32) Two coins are flipped. Find the probability that two heads are obtained.

33) The blood types of 100 donors are as follows:

10 have A positive blood type
12 have A negative blood type
18 have B positive blood type
20 have B negative blood type
25 have O blood type
15 have type AB blood.

If a donation from this group of donors is selected at random, what is the probability that this person has AB blood type?

34) A die is rolled and a coin is tossed. What is the probability that the die shows an even number and the coin shows tails?

35) A family is planning an annual picnic in Arizona. Rain is forecast for 45 days of the year, but when rain is forecast, the prediction is correct only 90% of the time. What is the probability that it will rain on the day of the picnic? Note that it is not a leap year.

Solutions – Data Analysis, Statistics, and Probability:

1) The correct answer is females over age 60. First look at the groups of dark grey bars, which represent males. Then look at the light grey bars, which are for the female population. You will see that the light grey bars for the 40 to 59 group are slightly lower than those of the 60 and over group. We can also clearly see that the first light grey bar in the age 60 and over group is the highest one of any of the bars. Adding this first light grey bar for cancer at 1,600 to the 220 for diabetes and the 20 for HIV, we arrive at 1,840 in total for all three diseases for females over age 60.

2) The charitable funding is the highest. You need to add up the three points, represented by the square, diamond, and triangle on each line, for each contributor (Private, State, Federal, Charitable, and Other). Here are the totals for the five contributors:
Private - 3,400
State - 3,800
Federal - 4,550
Charitable - 5,750
Other - 2,790
Therefore, the category of charitable is the highest.

3) The correct answer is the student union. Read the graph carefully, do the math, and then check your answers for questions like this one. The library equals 25%, the cafeteria is 18%, the student union is 29%, the sports center is 24%, and other facilities total 4%, so the student union is the highest.

4) The correct answer is 2240. Look at the data for retired couples and multiply: $56,000 \times .04 = 2240$

5) The correct answer is: 92.5

The arithmetic mean is just another way to say the average of a set of scores. The mean is calculated by dividing the total of all of the scores by the number of items in the set.

You need to find the total points for all the females and the total points for all the males. Then add these two amounts together and divide by the total number of students in the class to get your solution.

Females: $60 \times 95 = 5700$

Males: $60 \times 90 = 5400$

$(5700 + 5400) \div 120 = 11,100 \div 120 = 92.5$

6) The correct answer is: 72

First find the total points by taking Carmen's erroneous average times 4:

$4 \times 90 = 360$

Now divide the total points by the correct number of tests in order to get the correct average:

$360 \div 5 = 72$

7) The correct answer is: 21

The median is simply the middle value in the data set. First you have to put the numbers in the data set in the correct order from lowest to highest: 2, 8, 17, 21, 23, 24, 25. The median is the middle number in the set, which is 21 in this problem.

8) The correct answer is: 6.5

If there is an even number of items in the data set, such as eight cars in this problem, the median is the arithmetic mean or average of the two middle numbers. As in the previous problems, you need to put the numbers in the data set in order: 2, 5, 6, 7, 8, 10. The two values in the middle of the set are 6 and 7. Adding these together we get 13; then divide by 2 for the median. So 6.5 is the median for this problem.

9) The correct answer is: 1500

The mode is the number that appears the most frequently. For example, the number 3 appears four times in 1, 2, 3, 3, 3, 3, 7, 8, 8, 9. In our problem, 1500 is the only number in the data set that is repeated. Accordingly, 1500 is the mode since it is the number that appears most frequently.

10) The correct answer is: 1080 and 1582

We know that the mode is the number that appears most frequently, but in this problem the numbers 1080 and 1582 both appear two times. When this happens, we say that the data set is bimodal, and we assign two modes. Therefore, the modes for this problem are 1080 and 1582.

11) The correct answer is: no mode

What do we do when no number appears in the set more than once? If no number is duplicated, then we say that the data set has no mode. So there is no mode for the month of September.

12) The correct answer is: 21

The range is calculated by subtracting the minimum value in the data set from the maximum value in the data set. In other words, the range tells you the spread of the data. In this problem, the minimum value is 3 and the maximum value is 24. Therefore, the range is: 24 − 3 = 21

13) The correct answer is: 41.21

The variance measures the spread of the data around the arithmetic mean of the data set.

The variance of a data set is calculated in four steps:

Step 1 – Calculate the arithmetic mean for the data set.

Step 2 – Find the "difference from the mean" for each item in the data set by subtracting the mean from each value.

Step 3 – Square the "difference from the mean" for each item in the data set.

Step 4 – Calculate the mean of the squared figures derived from step 3 above to get the variance.

So let's complete each step for our weight loss group.

Step 1 – Calculate the arithmetic mean for the data set.

15 + 8 + 7 + 3 + 21 + 24 + 17 + 14 + 18 + 20 = 147 pounds lost in total for the entire group

147 divided by 10 group members equals an arithmetic mean of 14.7 for the data set.

Step 2 – Find the "difference from the mean" for each item in the data set by subtracting the mean from each value.

Subtract each value from the arithmetic mean.

Group member 1: 15 – 14.7 = 0.3
Group member 2: 8 – 14.7 = –6.7
Group member 3: 7 – 14.7 = –7.7
Group member 4: 3 – 14.7 = –11.7
Group member 5: 21 – 14.7 = 6.3
Group member 6: 24 – 14.7 = 9.3
Group member 7: 17 – 14.7 = 2.3
Group member 8: 14 – 14.7 = –0.7
Group member 9: 18 – 14.7 = 3.3
Group member 10: 20 – 14.7 = 5.3

Step 3 – Square the "difference from the mean" for each item in the data set.

Group member 1: $0.3^2 = 0.09$
Group member 2: $–6.7^2 = 44.89$
Group member 3: $–7.7^2 = 59.29$
Group member 4: $–11.7^2 = 136.89$
Group member 5: $6.3^2 = 39.69$
Group member 6: $9.3^2 = 86.49$
Group member 7: $2.3^2 = 5.29$
Group member 8: $–0.7^2 = 0.49$
Group member 9: $3.3^2 = 10.89$
Group member 10: $5.3^2 = 28.09$

Step 4 – Calculate the mean of the squared figures derived from step 3 above to get the variance.

0.09 + 44.89 + 59.29 + 136.89 + 39.69 + 86.49 + 5.29 + 0.49 + 10.89 + 28.09 = 412.10

412.10 ÷ 10 = 41.21

In other words, 412.10 divided by 10 equals a variance of 41.21

14) The correct answer is: 6.42

The standard deviation of a data set measures the spread of the data around the mean of the data set.

The standard deviation is calculated by taking the square root of the variance.

In the problem above our variance was 41.21

So the standard deviation for the weight loss group is the square root of 41.21, which is 6.42

15) The correct answer is: 6

The standard deviation is useful because you can see which members of the group are within one standard deviation from the mean.

The standard deviation measurement therefore indicates the level of "normality" or "abnormality" of each of the items in the data set.

The arithmetic mean for our group was 14.7

The standard deviation was 6.42

So the members that are within one standard deviation of the mean will include those that are one standard deviation above the mean:

14.7 + 6.42 = 21.12

The members that are within one standard deviation of the mean will also include those that are one standard deviation below the mean:

14.7 − 6.42 = 8.28

So we have to find group members whose weight loss amounts are between 8.28 and 21.12

The weight loss amounts for each group member were as follows:

Group member 1: 15
Group member 2: 8
Group member 3: 7
Group member 4: 3
Group member 5: 21
Group member 6: 24
Group member 7: 17
Group member 8: 14
Group member 9: 18
Group member 10: 20

The weight loss amounts for group members 1, 5, 7, 8, 9, and 10 are between 8.28 and 21.12

So there are 6 members of the group within one standard deviation of the mean.

16) The correct answer is: 318.8542

We have the chance to practice calculating variance with a different data set in this problem. You will remember that the variance of a data set is calculated in four steps:

Step 1 – Calculate the arithmetic mean for the data set.

Using the data for the 12 students in our problem above:

96 + 99 + 97 + 98 + 64 + 59 + 83 + 79 + 67 + 44 + 72 + 57 = 915

915 ÷ 12 = 76.25

So 76.25 is the arithmetic mean.

Step 2 – Find the "difference from the mean" for each item in the data set by subtracting the mean from each value.

Student 1:   96 – 76.25 = 19.75
Student 2:   99 – 76.25 = 22.75
Student 3:   97 – 76.25 = 20.75
Student 4:   98 – 76.25 = 21.75
Student 5:   64 – 76.25 = –12.25
Student 6:   59 – 76.25 = –17.25
Student 7:   83 – 76.25 = 6.75
Student 8:   79 – 76.25 = 2.75
Student 9:   67 – 76.25 = –9.25
Student 10:   44 – 76.25 = –32.25
Student 11:   72 – 76.25 = –4.25
Student 12:   57 – 76.25 = –19.25

Step 3 – Square the "difference from the mean" for each item in the data set.

Student 1: 19.75^2 = 390.0625
Student 2: 22.75^2 = 517.5625
Student 3: 20.75^2 = 430.5625
Student 4: 21.75^2 = 473.0625
Student 5: $–12.25^2$ = 150.0625
Student 6: $–17.25^2$ = 297.5625
Student 7: 6.75^2 = 45.5625
Student 8: 2.75^2 = 7.5625
Student 9: $–9.25^2$ = 85.5625
Student 10: $–32.25^2$ = 1040.0625
Student 11: $–4.25^2$ = 18.0625
Student 12: $–19.25^2$ = 370.5625

Step 4 – Calculate the mean of the squared figures derived from step 3 above to get the variance.

390.0625 + 517.5625 + 430.5625 + 473.0625 + 150.0625 + 297.5625 + 45.5625 + 7.5625 + 85.5625 + 1040.0625 + 18.0625 + 370.5625 = 3826.25

3826.25 ÷ 12 = 318.8542

17) The correct answer is: 17.8565

We have to find the square root of 318.8542, which is 17.8565

So our standard deviation is 17.8565

18) The correct answer is: 104,000

The lowest income is 31,000 and the highest is 135,000.

The range is the difference between the low and the high:

135,000 – 31,000 = 104,000

So the range is 104,000.

19) The correct answer is: 5%

Remember that the median is the middle figure.

First put the amounts in order: –3%, –2%, 1.3%, 5%, 7.5%, 14%, 17%

So the median is 5%.

20) The correct answer is: 5.69%

Take all of the percentages, add them up, and divide by 7:

–2% + 5% + 7.5% + 14% + 17% + 1.3% + –3% = 39.8 ÷ 7 = 5.69%

21) The correct answer is: 368

Step 1 – Calculate the arithmetic mean for the data set.

5,250 + 5,299 + 5,275 + 5,300 + 5,295 = 26,419

26,419 ÷ 5 = 5284

Step 2 – Find the "difference from the mean" for each item in the data set by subtracting the mean from each value.

91

Car 1: 5250 – 5284 = –34
Car 2: 5299 – 5284 = 15
Car 3: 5275 – 5284 = –9
Car 4: 5300 – 5284 = 16
Car 5: 5295 – 5284 = 11

Step 3 – Square the "difference from the mean" for each item in the data set.

Car 1: -34^2 = 1156
Car 2: 15^2 = 225
Car 3: -9^2 = 81
Car 4: 16^2 = 256
Car 5: 11^2 = 121

Step 4 – Calculate the mean of the squared figures derived from step 3 above to get the variance.

1156 + 225 + 81 + 256 +121 = 1839

1839 ÷ 5 = 368

22) The correct answer is: 19.18

The square root of 368 is 19.18.

Therefore, the standard deviation is 19.18.

23) The correct answer is: 4

The mean was 5284.

So cars that are one standard deviation above the mean are valued at: 5284 + 19 = 5303

Cars that are one standard deviation below the mean are valued at: 5284 – 19 = 5265

The values of the cars were:

Car 1: $5,250
Car 2: $5,299
Car 3: $5,275
Car 4: $5,300
Car 5: $5,295

The value of car 1 is less than $5,265, so four cars are within one standard deviation of the mean.

24) The correct answer is: 86 or higher

The percentile for an observation x is found by dividing the number of observations less than x by the total number of observations and then multiplying this quantity by 100.

First find out how many students had scores less than 85.

50 – 5 = 45

Then divide this result by the total.

45/50 = 90%

If a student had a score of 86 or above, he or she was in the 90th percentile.

25) The correct answers are: A and C

A probability is always greater than or equal to 0 and less than or equal to 1. So A and C cannot represent probabilities.

26) The correct answer is: 50%

For probability problems, your first step is to calculate how many items there are in total.

So, first of all, you need to calculate how many items there are in the entire set:

4 + 6 + 10 = 20

Then calculate the probability by placing the white marbles in the numerator and the total marbles in the denominator:

10 / 20 = 50%

27) The correct answer is: 20%

Here we have 3 blue scarves, 1 red scarf, 5 green scarves, and 2 orange scarves, so we have 11 scarves in total.

Deduct the amount that has been taken away. In this problem, one scarf has been removed, so there are 10 scarves remaining.

Since the scarf that was removed was red, there are still 2 orange scarves.

The probability is expressed as a fraction with the remaining chances as the numerator and the remaining total as the denominator, in other words $^2/_{10}$ for this problem.

Finally, we convert this to a percentage: $^2/_{10}$ = 20%

28) The correct answer is: 1.9%

There are 52 cards in a deck of cards. There is only one ace.

So the probability is 1 / 52 = 1.9%

29) The correct answer is: 23%

There are 4 kings, 4 queens, and 4 jacks in a deck of card, for a total of 12.

So the probability is 12 / 52 = 3 / 13 = 23%

30) The correct answer is: 16.67%

For more complex probability problems like this one, you need two concepts: "sample space" and "event of interest."

We will have S represent the sample space and E will represent the event of interest.

n(S) is the number of items in the sample space and n(E) is the number of items in the event.

The sample space S for the question for tossing the dice is the list of the possible combinations that can be obtained from the sum of dots on the two dice. Since each die has numbers 1 to 6, the sample space is:

S = { (1,1),(1,2),(1,3),(1,4),(1,5),(1,6)
    (2,1),(2,2),(2,3),(2,4),(2,5),(2,6)
    (3,1),(3,2),(3,3),(3,4),(3,5),(3,6)
    (4,1),(4,2),(4,3),(4,4),(4,5),(4,6)
    (5,1),(5,2),(5,3),(5,4),(5,5),(5,6)
    (6,1),(6,2),(6,3),(6,4),(6,5),(6,6) }

In other words, there are 36 possible outcomes if we count each individual combination above, so there are 36 items in the sample space.

The event is that "a sum greater than 9 will be obtained," so write down the possible combinations that equal 10 or more from the two dice.

E = {(4,6);(5,5);(5,6);(6,4);(6,5);(6,6)}

So there are 6 possible events.

Now use the formula for probability.

P(E) = n(E) / n(S)

In other words, the probability of event E is calculated by dividing the event into the sample space.

Here we have a sample space of 36 items and an event of 6.

(P)E = 6 / 36 = 1 / 6 = 16.67%

31) The correct answer is: 8.33%

Remember that the sample space S for the question for tossing the dice is the list of the possible numbers that can be obtained from the sum of dots on the two dice.

The sample space for this question is:

S = { (1,1),(1,2),(1,3),(1,4),(1,5),(1,6)
     (2,1),(2,2),(2,3),(2,4),(2,5),(2,6)
     (3,1),(3,2),(3,3),(3,4),(3,5),(3,6)
     (4,1),(4,2),(4,3),(4,4),(4,5),(4,6)
     (5,1),(5,2),(5,3),(5,4),(5,5),(5,6)
     (6,1),(6,2),(6,3),(6,4),(6,5),(6,6) }

The event is that "number less than 4 will be obtained" so write down the possible results.

E = {(1,1);(1,2);(2,1)}

Now use the formula for probability.

P(E) = n(E) / n(S)

Here we have a sample space of 36 items and an event of 3.

(P)E = 3 / 36 = 1 / 12 = 8.33%

32) The correct answer is: 25%

Each coin has two possible outcomes H (heads) and T (Tails).

The sample space S for flipping the coins is the list of the possible outcomes that can be obtained from the combinations of the two sides of the two coins. The sample space is:

S = {H & H, T & T, H & T, T & H}

The event is that "two heads are obtained."

E = {H & H}

Now use the formula for probability.

P(E) = n(E) / n(S)

Here we have a sample space of 4 and an event of 1.

(P)E = 1 / 4 = 25%

33) The correct answer is: 15%

The sample set is 100 donors.

There are 15 possible outcomes for the event.

So the probability is 15 / 100 = 15%

34) The correct answer is: 25%

The sample space is as follows:

S = { (1,H),(2,H),(3,H),(4,H),(5,H),(6,H)
      (1,T),(2,T),(3,T),(4,T),(5,T),(6,T)}

The event is that "the die shows an even number and the coin shows a tails."

The event is:

E={(2,T),(4,T),(6,T)}

So the probability is:

P(E) = n(E) / n(S) = 3 / 12 = 1 / 4 = 25%

35) The correct answer is: 10.8%

The sample space is defined by the chance of rain.

In terms of probabilities, we know that there are 365 days in non-leap years, so this goes in the denominator. The chance of rain goes in the numerator:

P(E) = 45 / 365 = 12%

However, when rain is forecast, the prediction is correct only 90 percent of the time.

P(E) = 45 / 365 = 12% × 90% = 10.8%

Made in the USA
Lexington, KY
15 June 2014